From Idea to Empire

Innovative Techniques to Propel Your Company to Success

TAYLOR TRIVETT

The presentation of the information is without contract or any type of guarantee assurance. The trademarks that are used are without any consent, and the publication of the trademark is without permission or backing by the trademark owner. All trademarks and brands within this book are for clarifying purposes only and are the owned by the owners themselves, not affiliated with this document.

Table of Contents

Chapter 1

Introduction to Business Strategies

Understanding Business Strategy

Understanding business strategy is essential for any company aiming for long-term success and sustainability. At its core, business strategy is about making choices—choices about what markets to enter, what products to offer, how to allocate resources, and how to differentiate from competitors. These choices shape a company's direction and influence every aspect of its operations.

A solid business strategy begins with a clear understanding of what strategy itself entails. Strategy is not merely a plan or a set of goals; it is a coherent response to the challenges and opportunities that a company faces. It involves setting a direction, making decisions that are consistent with that direction, and ensuring that all parts of the organization are aligned with these decisions.

One of the critical aspects of formulating a business strategy is understanding the competitive landscape. This involves a thorough analysis of the market and the industry in which the company operates. Market analysis helps identify potential opportunities and threats, enabling a company to position itself effectively. It involves examining market trends, customer needs, and competitor actions. By understanding these elements, a company can develop strategies that cater to unmet needs or exploit gaps in the market.

Strategic planning is another fundamental component. This is the process by which a company defines its strategy and decides how to allocate resources to pursue it. A well-crafted strategic plan outlines the company's vision, mission, and objectives. It also details the specific actions needed to achieve these objectives, the resources required, and the timelines involved. Effective strategic planning requires a thorough understanding of the company's strengths and weaknesses, as well as the external opportunities and threats it faces.

Setting clear objectives is crucial for any business strategy. Objectives provide direction and a sense of purpose, guiding the actions of the organization. They should be specific, measurable, achievable, relevant, and time-bound (SMART). Clear objectives help ensure that everyone in the organization understands what the company is trying to achieve and can work towards these goals in a coordinated manner.

Aligning strategies with company goals is another key element. This means ensuring that all strategic decisions and actions support the overall objectives of the organization. It requires a holistic approach where departments and teams work together towards common goals rather than pursuing their own isolated agendas. Alignment also involves regular communication and coordination among different parts of the organization to ensure that everyone is on the same page.

Flexibility is an essential characteristic of a successful business strategy. In a constantly changing business environment, a rigid strategy can become obsolete quickly. Companies need to be able to adapt their strategies in response to new information, changing market conditions, and emerging opportunities or threats. This requires a willingness to regularly review and adjust the strategy as necessary, ensuring it remains relevant and effective.

Risk management is another vital component of business strategy. Every strategic decision carries some level of risk, and managing these risks is crucial for long-term success. This involves identifying potential risks, assessing their likelihood and impact, and developing strategies to mitigate them. Effective risk management helps ensure that the company can navigate uncertainties and continue to thrive even in adverse conditions.

Resource allocation is a critical aspect of strategy implementation. Resources—whether financial, human, or technological—are limited, and how they are allocated can significantly impact the success of a strategy. Strategic resource allocation involves prioritizing initiatives that are most likely to achieve the company's objectives and ensuring that these initiatives have the necessary resources to succeed. This requires careful planning and ongoing monitoring to ensure that resources are being used effectively and efficiently.

Leadership plays a crucial role in the success of a business strategy. Effective leaders provide direction, inspire and motivate employees, and ensure that the organization stays focused on its strategic objectives. They also play a key role in fostering a culture that supports the strategy, encouraging innovation, collaboration, and continuous improvement. Strong leadership helps ensure that the strategy is implemented effectively and that the organization can adapt to changing conditions.

Communication is another critical factor in the success of a business strategy. Clear, consistent communication helps ensure that everyone in the organization understands the strategy, their role in it, and how their efforts contribute to achieving the company's goals. This involves not only top-down communication, where leaders communicate the strategy to employees, but also bottom-up communication, where employees can provide feedback and insights that can help refine and improve the strategy.

Monitoring and evaluating the implementation of a strategy is essential to ensure its success. This involves tracking progress against the objectives, assessing the effectiveness of actions taken, and making adjustments as necessary. Regular monitoring helps identify any issues or obstacles early, allowing the company to address them before they become significant problems. It also provides an opportunity to celebrate successes and learn from failures, continuously improving the strategy and its implementation.

A successful business strategy is not a one-time effort but an ongoing process. It requires continuous attention, regular review, and a willingness to adapt and evolve. By understanding the fundamental principles of business strategy and effectively applying them, companies can position themselves for long-term success, navigating the complexities of the business environment and achieving their strategic objectives.

In summary, understanding business strategy involves recognizing it as a coherent response to market challenges, setting clear and aligned objectives, being flexible, managing risks effectively, allocating resources strategically, and ensuring strong leadership and communication. By mastering these elements, a company can develop and implement strategies that drive success and sustain competitive advantage in an ever-changing business landscape.

Another crucial aspect of understanding business strategy is the concept of competitive advantage. Competitive advantage refers to what sets a company apart from its competitors and allows it to generate greater value for its customers. This can be achieved through various means, such as cost leadership, differentiation, or focus strategies.

The Importance of Strategic Planning

Strategic planning is the blueprint for achieving a company's long-term vision and goals. It provides a structured approach to navigating the complexities of the business environment, enabling organizations to anticipate changes, allocate resources efficiently, and ensure that all efforts are aligned toward common objectives. The importance of strategic planning cannot be overstated, as it serves as the foundation for sustainable growth and competitive advantage.

At the heart of strategic planning is the need to clearly define an organization's direction. This begins with articulating a compelling vision and mission statement. The vision statement outlines what the organization aspires to be in the future, while the mission statement describes its purpose and the core activities it undertakes to achieve that vision. These statements provide a north star for the organization, guiding decision-making and inspiring employees.

Once the vision and mission are established, the next step in strategic planning is to conduct a thorough analysis of the internal and external environments. Internally, this involves assessing the company's strengths and weaknesses. Strengths are the internal capabilities that give the company an advantage, such as proprietary technology, skilled workforce, or strong brand reputation. Weaknesses, on the other hand, are areas where the company is at a disadvantage, such as limited resources, outdated systems, or gaps in expertise.

Externally, the analysis focuses on identifying opportunities and threats in the market. Opportunities are favorable conditions in the external environment that the company can exploit to achieve its goals. These might include emerging markets, technological advancements, or shifts in consumer behavior. Threats are external factors that could hinder the company's progress, such as economic downturns, regulatory changes, or competitive pressures. This comprehensive analysis, often referred to as a SWOT analysis (Strengths, Weaknesses, Opportunities, Threats), provides a clear picture of the current landscape and helps in formulating strategies that leverage strengths, mitigate weaknesses, capitalize on opportunities, and guard against threats.

Setting strategic objectives is the next critical step in the planning process. Objectives should be specific, measurable, achievable, relevant, and time-bound (SMART). Clear objectives provide a roadmap for the organization, breaking down the vision into actionable steps. For instance, if a company's vision is to become a market leader in sustainable products, a strategic objective might be to increase the market share of its eco-friendly product line by 20% within the next three years.

Resource allocation is another fundamental aspect of strategic planning. Resources include not only financial capital but also human capital, technology, and time. Effective resource allocation ensures that the company's most critical initiatives are adequately funded and staffed. This often involves making tough decisions about where to invest and where to cut back. Prioritizing initiatives that align most closely with the strategic objectives is key to maximizing impact and avoiding the dilution of efforts.

A well-crafted strategic plan also includes a detailed action plan. This plan outlines the specific actions needed to achieve each strategic objective, along with timelines, responsible parties, and key performance indicators (KPIs) to measure progress. Action plans serve as a bridge between high-level strategy and day-to-day operations, ensuring that everyone in the organization understands their role in executing the strategy.

One of the most challenging aspects of strategic planning is managing change. Implementing a new strategy often requires significant changes in processes, systems, and sometimes even culture. Change management is essential to ensure that these transitions are smooth and that employees are on board. Effective communication is crucial, as it helps build understanding and buy-in across the organization. Leaders must clearly articulate the reasons for the change, the benefits it will bring, and how it aligns with the company's vision and mission.

Monitoring and evaluating progress is vital to the success of any strategic plan. This involves regularly reviewing performance against the established KPIs and making adjustments as needed. The business environment is dynamic, and unforeseen challenges and opportunities can arise. Regular monitoring allows the organization to stay agile and responsive, making data-driven decisions to stay on course. This iterative process of planning, executing, monitoring, and adjusting helps ensure that the strategy remains relevant and effective over time.

Strategic planning also fosters a proactive rather than reactive approach to business management. Companies that engage in strategic planning are better prepared to anticipate and respond to changes in the market. They can identify trends early, adjust their strategies accordingly, and maintain a competitive edge. This proactive stance is particularly important in today's fast-paced business environment, where technological advancements and shifting consumer preferences can quickly disrupt industries.

Moreover, strategic planning enhances organizational alignment and cohesion. When everyone in the organization understands the strategic direction and their role in achieving it, there is greater coordination and collaboration. This alignment helps break down silos, encourages cross-functional teamwork, and ensures that all efforts are directed toward common goals. It also boosts employee engagement and morale, as individuals can see how their work contributes to the bigger picture.

Effective strategic planning also involves considering different scenarios and developing contingency plans. Scenario planning helps organizations anticipate various future states and prepare for them. By considering best-case, worst-case, and most likely scenarios, companies can develop flexible strategies that are robust under different conditions. This preparedness reduces uncertainty and enhances the organization's ability to navigate volatility.

Leadership plays a critical role in the strategic planning process. Leaders must champion the strategic planning efforts, providing direction, support, and resources. They must also be willing to make difficult decisions, such as reallocating resources, discontinuing underperforming initiatives, or investing in new areas. Strong leadership ensures that the strategic plan is not just a document but a living guide that shapes daily actions and decisions.

In conclusion, strategic planning is essential for achieving long-term success and sustainability. It involves defining a clear direction, conducting a thorough analysis of the internal and external environments, setting SMART objectives, allocating resources effectively, developing detailed action plans, managing change, and continuously monitoring and adjusting strategies. Through strategic planning, organizations can navigate the complexities of the business environment, align efforts toward common goals, and maintain a competitive advantage. The importance of strategic planning lies in its ability to provide a structured approach to achieving the company's vision and ensuring sustainable growth in an ever-changing world.

Strategic planning also plays a crucial role in risk management. By identifying potential risks early in the planning process, organizations can develop strategies to mitigate these risks before they become significant issues. This proactive approach to risk management helps ensure that the company is prepared for unexpected challenges and can continue to operate smoothly even in the face of adversity. Contingency planning, as part of the overall strategic plan, outlines specific actions that will be taken if certain risks materialize. This level of preparedness can be the difference between a minor setback and a major crisis.

Types of Business Strategies

Business strategies are the cornerstone of organizational success, providing a roadmap for achieving competitive advantage and long-term sustainability. Understanding the various types of business strategies is essential for any entrepreneur or manager seeking to steer their company toward growth and profitability. Each strategy offers unique benefits and is suited to different business contexts and goals. By exploring these strategies, you can determine which approach aligns best with your organization's vision and market conditions.

One of the most common types of business strategies is the cost leadership strategy. Companies that adopt this approach aim to become the lowest-cost producer in their industry. By minimizing production costs, these companies can offer their products or services at lower prices than their competitors, attracting price-sensitive customers and increasing market share. Achieving cost leadership often involves optimizing operational efficiency, leveraging economies of scale, and implementing strict cost control measures. Famous examples include Walmart and Southwest Airlines, which have built their success on providing value to customers through low prices.

In contrast to cost leadership, a differentiation strategy focuses on creating unique products or services that offer distinct benefits to customers. Companies pursuing differentiation aim to stand out in the market by delivering superior quality, innovative features, exceptional service, or a strong brand identity. This strategy allows businesses to charge premium prices, as customers perceive the added value and are willing to pay more. Apple exemplifies the differentiation strategy with its innovative technology and sleek design, which have cultivated a loyal customer base willing to pay higher prices for its products.

Another effective approach is the focus strategy, which involves targeting a specific market segment or niche. Companies adopting a focus strategy concentrate their efforts on serving the unique needs of a particular group of customers, rather than trying to appeal to the broader market. This allows them to tailor their products, services, and marketing efforts to better meet the demands of their chosen segment, often leading to higher customer satisfaction and loyalty. There are two main types of focus strategies: cost focus and differentiation focus. In cost focus, a company aims to be the lowest-cost provider within its niche, while in differentiation focus, the company offers specialized products or services that cater to the specific preferences of its target market. An example of a focus strategy is Rolls-Royce, which targets the luxury automobile market with highly customized, premium vehicles.

A growth strategy is another important type of business strategy, aimed at increasing the company's market share, revenue, or overall size. Growth strategies can be implemented through various means, such as expanding product lines, entering new markets, or acquiring other businesses. Organic growth involves expanding the company's existing operations by increasing output, enhancing marketing efforts, or developing new products. Inorganic growth, on the other hand, involves mergers, acquisitions, or strategic partnerships to quickly gain market share or capabilities. Starbucks has successfully employed a growth strategy by continuously opening new stores and expanding its product offerings to include items like teas, sandwiches, and bakery goods.

Diversification is a strategy where a company expands into new markets or product lines that are distinct from its core business. This approach can help spread risk by reducing dependence on a single market or product. Diversification can be related or unrelated. Related diversification involves entering a new market or product line that has some connection to the company's existing business, such as sharing technology, distribution channels, or customers. Unrelated diversification, in contrast, involves venturing into entirely different industries. A classic example of related diversification is Disney, which has expanded from animated movies into theme parks, merchandise, and television networks. General Electric, on the other hand, exemplifies unrelated diversification by operating in diverse industries such as aviation, healthcare, and financial services.

Innovation strategy focuses on developing new products, services, or processes that create significant value for customers and differentiate the company from competitors. Companies that adopt an innovation strategy invest heavily in research and development to pioneer breakthrough technologies or business models. This strategy can lead to first-mover advantages, allowing the company to establish a strong market position before competitors can catch up. Tesla is a prime example of an innovation strategy, revolutionizing the automotive industry with its electric vehicles and autonomous driving technology.

A competitive strategy is designed to outperform rivals and achieve a superior market position. Michael Porter's generic strategies framework outlines three primary competitive strategies: cost leadership, differentiation, and focus, as previously discussed. However, companies can also adopt hybrid strategies that combine elements of these approaches. For instance, a company might pursue cost leadership in certain segments while differentiating its products in others. Toyota has successfully implemented a hybrid strategy by offering affordable, high-quality vehicles across various market segments, from economy to luxury.

A defensive strategy aims to protect the company's market position and competitive advantage from external threats. This can involve actions such as strengthening customer loyalty, improving operational efficiency, or enhancing product quality to fend off competitors. Defensive strategies are particularly important in mature markets where growth opportunities are limited, and companies must focus on maintaining their existing customer base. Coca-Cola employs a defensive strategy by continuously investing in brand marketing, expanding its product portfolio, and optimizing its distribution network to maintain its dominant position in the beverage industry.

Another strategic approach is the turnaround strategy, which is employed when a company is facing significant challenges or declining performance. The goal of a turnaround strategy is to stabilize the business, address underlying issues, and return to profitability. This often involves cost-cutting measures, restructuring operations, divesting non-core assets, or revitalizing the company's product offerings. A notable example of a successful turnaround strategy is Ford Motor Company, which, under the leadership of CEO Alan Mulally, restructured its operations, streamlined its product lineup, and focused on improving quality and efficiency to recover from financial distress.

A retrenchment strategy involves reducing the scale or scope of a company's operations to improve financial stability and focus on core activities. This can include downsizing, closing unprofitable divisions, or withdrawing from certain markets. Retrenchment strategies are often used when a company is experiencing financial difficulties or when it needs to refocus on its core competencies. Hewlett-Packard (HP) implemented a retrenchment strategy by splitting into two separate companies, HP Inc. and Hewlett Packard Enterprise, to streamline operations and concentrate on their respective strengths in personal computing and enterprise solutions.

Global strategies are designed for companies looking to expand their operations internationally. These strategies involve tailoring products, marketing, and operations to different geographic markets while leveraging global efficiencies. There are three primary types of global strategies: multi-domestic, global, and transnational. A multi-domestic strategy involves customizing products and marketing efforts to suit local preferences and conditions. A global strategy focuses on standardizing products and marketing to achieve economies of scale. A transnational strategy seeks to balance global efficiency with local responsiveness by integrating and coordinating activities across different countries. McDonald's employs a transnational strategy by maintaining a consistent brand image and core menu items globally while adapting to local tastes and preferences.

Understanding these various types of business strategies equips entrepreneurs and managers with the tools to navigate complex market dynamics, capitalize on opportunities, and achieve sustained success. The key is to carefully analyze the company's internal capabilities, market conditions, and competitive landscape to select the strategy that best aligns with the organization's goals and vision. By doing so, businesses can position themselves for growth, resilience, and long-term profitability.

In addition to understanding and implementing various business strategies, it is crucial for organizations to continuously monitor and adapt their strategies in response to changing market conditions and internal dynamics. This iterative process, often referred to as strategic management, ensures that the business remains agile and responsive to new opportunities and threats.

Setting Clear Objectives

Clear objectives are the foundation upon which successful businesses are built. They guide decision-making, align team efforts, and provide measurable benchmarks for progress. Without well-defined objectives, organizations risk drifting aimlessly, wasting resources, and missing opportunities for growth and improvement. Setting clear objectives is not just a strategic exercise; it's a critical practice that influences every aspect of a business.

The first step in setting clear objectives is understanding the importance of specificity. Vague goals like "increase sales" or "improve customer satisfaction" lack the precision needed to drive focused action. Instead, objectives should be SMART: Specific, Measurable, Achievable, Relevant, and Time-bound. For instance, an objective like "increase online sales by 20% within the next six months" provides a clear target and timeframe, making it easier to devise strategies and monitor progress.

Specificity in objectives helps break down broad goals into smaller, actionable steps. For example, if a company aims to expand its market share, it might set specific objectives related to product development, marketing campaigns, or customer service enhancements. Each of these areas can then be further broken down into detailed tasks and milestones, ensuring that every aspect of the goal is addressed systematically.

Measurability is another crucial aspect of setting clear objectives. Without quantifiable criteria, it's impossible to track progress or determine success. Measurable objectives allow businesses to use data and metrics to assess their performance. For instance, if the objective is to improve customer satisfaction, the company might use customer feedback surveys, net promoter scores, or repeat purchase rates as indicators of progress. These metrics provide tangible evidence of whether the strategies implemented are effective or need adjustment.

Achievability ensures that objectives are realistic and attainable given the organization's resources and constraints. Setting overly ambitious goals can be demotivating and lead to burnout, while too-easily attainable objectives might not drive the necessary growth or improvement. Achievable objectives strike a balance, challenging the organization without setting it up for failure. For instance, a startup might aim for a 10% growth in its user base within the first year, considering its current capabilities and market conditions.

Relevance ties objectives to the broader mission and vision of the organization. Relevant objectives ensure that every goal supports the company's overall strategic direction. This alignment helps prioritize efforts and resources, focusing on what truly matters for long-term success. For example, if a company's mission is to lead in sustainable products, its objectives might include reducing carbon emissions in production or sourcing materials from eco-friendly suppliers. These objectives not only advance the company's mission but also resonate with its values and customer expectations.

Time-bound objectives create a sense of urgency and provide deadlines for achieving goals. Without a clear timeframe, objectives can languish indefinitely, leading to procrastination and lack of focus. Time-bound objectives encourage timely action and regular review of progress. For instance, setting a deadline to launch a new product within the next quarter ensures that the team works diligently to meet that target, breaking down the project into manageable phases and setting interim deadlines.

Once objectives are set, communicating them effectively to the entire organization is crucial. Clear communication ensures that everyone understands the goals, their importance, and their role in achieving them. This can be done through team meetings, internal newsletters, or digital dashboards that track progress. Transparency in communication fosters a sense of shared purpose and accountability, motivating employees to contribute their best efforts toward the common goals.

Another essential aspect of setting clear objectives is involving key stakeholders in the goal-setting process. When team members participate in defining objectives, they are more likely to feel ownership and commitment to achieving them. This collaborative approach also leverages diverse perspectives and expertise, leading to more comprehensive and realistic objectives. For example, involving sales, marketing, and product development teams in setting revenue targets ensures that the goals consider market conditions, customer needs, and the company's capabilities.

Regular review and adjustment of objectives are necessary to respond to changing circumstances and ensure continued relevance. Business environments are dynamic, and objectives that were set at the beginning of the year might need to be revised as new opportunities or challenges arise. Regular check-ins, such as quarterly reviews, allow organizations to assess progress, celebrate achievements, and make necessary adjustments. This iterative process keeps objectives aligned with the current reality and maintains momentum toward achieving them.

Setting clear objectives also involves anticipating potential obstacles and planning for contingencies. Identifying risks and developing mitigation strategies ensures that the organization is prepared to tackle challenges without derailing progress. For instance, if a company aims to expand into a new market, it might anticipate regulatory hurdles or supply chain disruptions and devise plans to address these issues proactively.

In addition to organizational objectives, setting individual and team objectives is vital for personal accountability and professional growth. When employees have clear, personalized goals that align with the company's objectives, they are more motivated and focused. Performance appraisals and development plans should be tied to these individual and team objectives, providing a clear framework for career progression and recognition. For example, a sales representative might have an objective to achieve a certain number of new client acquisitions each quarter, with incentives tied to meeting or exceeding these targets.

Leadership plays a critical role in setting and reinforcing clear objectives. Leaders must articulate the vision, inspire the team, and provide the resources and support necessary to achieve the goals. This includes removing barriers, offering guidance, and recognizing achievements. Effective leaders also model the commitment and focus required to meet objectives, setting an example for the entire organization.

Furthermore, technology can be a powerful ally in setting and tracking clear objectives. Project management tools, performance dashboards, and data analytics platforms provide real-time insights into progress, helping teams stay on track and make informed decisions. These tools can automate reporting, highlight areas needing attention, and facilitate communication across the organization. For instance, a digital dashboard that tracks sales performance against targets can quickly identify trends, allowing for timely interventions.

Incentives and rewards linked to achieving objectives can significantly boost motivation and performance. Recognizing and rewarding employees for meeting or exceeding their goals reinforces the importance of clear objectives and encourages a culture of achievement. These incentives can be financial, such as bonuses or raises, or non-financial, such as public recognition, additional vacation days, or professional development opportunities.

Finally, celebrating milestones and successes along the way keeps the team motivated and reinforces the value of clear objectives. Recognizing progress, no matter how small, builds momentum and fosters a positive, achievement-oriented culture. This celebration can take many forms, from team meetings and email shout-outs to formal award ceremonies.

Setting clear objectives is a multifaceted process that requires thoughtful planning, effective communication, ongoing review, and strong leadership. By ensuring that objectives are specific, measurable, achievable, relevant, and time-bound, organizations can navigate the complexities of the business environment with greater focus and confidence. Clear objectives provide a roadmap for success, aligning efforts, driving action, and measuring progress, ultimately leading to sustained growth and achievement.

Additionally, clear objectives serve as a critical tool for decision-making and prioritization. In the day-to-day operations of a business, countless decisions must be made, ranging from resource allocation to tactical adjustments. When objectives are well-defined, they act as a guiding star, helping leaders and employees determine which actions will most effectively drive the organization toward its goals. For example, if an objective is to enter a new market within the next year, decisions about marketing budgets, product development, and staffing can be more easily aligned with this priority.

Aligning Strategies with Company Goals

Aligning strategies with company goals is paramount for any organization aiming to achieve sustained success. This alignment ensures that every action taken, resource allocated, and decision made is directly contributing to the overarching objectives of the business. It provides a cohesive framework that binds the various functions and efforts within the organization, creating a unified direction and purpose.

The process begins with a thorough understanding of the company's goals. These goals are typically articulated in the company's mission and vision statements, strategic plans, and key performance indicators (KPIs). They reflect the long-term aspirations and the desired position of the company in its market or industry. For example, a company's goal might be to become the market leader in renewable energy solutions within the next decade. This goal sets the stage for all strategic initiatives and operational plans.

Once the goals are clear, the next step is to develop strategies that are not only aligned with these goals but also feasible and effective. This involves a deep dive into the company's strengths, weaknesses, opportunities, and threats (SWOT analysis). By understanding these internal and external factors, the company can craft strategies that leverage its strengths, mitigate its weaknesses, capitalize on opportunities, and guard against threats. For instance, a company with strong research and development capabilities might focus on innovation as a key strategy to achieve its goal of market leadership in renewable energy.

Communication plays a crucial role in the alignment process. It is essential that everyone in the organization, from top management to front-line employees, understands the company's goals and the strategies designed to achieve them. Clear, consistent, and transparent communication ensures that all employees are on the same page and working towards the same objectives. This can be achieved through regular town hall meetings, internal newsletters, strategic planning sessions, and performance reviews. For example, a quarterly town hall meeting where the CEO outlines the company's progress towards its goals and the strategies being implemented can reinforce alignment and motivate employees.

Implementing aligned strategies requires meticulous planning and resource allocation. Each strategy should have a detailed action plan that outlines specific tasks, timelines, responsible parties, and required resources. This ensures that everyone involved knows what needs to be done, by whom, and when. It also facilitates monitoring and evaluation, allowing the company to track progress and make necessary adjustments. For instance, if a strategy involves launching a new product, the action plan might include market research, product development, marketing campaigns, and sales training, each with specific deadlines and assigned teams.

Monitoring and evaluation are critical components of strategy implementation. Regular tracking of progress against the action plan and KPIs helps identify any deviations or issues early on, allowing for timely corrective actions. It also provides insights into what is working well and what might need to be adjusted. For example, if sales figures are not meeting targets, the company might need to revisit its marketing strategy or provide additional training to its sales team. Continuous feedback loops and performance reviews help keep the strategy aligned with the company's goals.

Flexibility and adaptability are also key in aligning strategies with company goals. The business environment is dynamic, and unexpected changes can occur. It is important for companies to remain agile and be ready to pivot their strategies when necessary. This does not mean abandoning the original goals but rather finding new ways to achieve them in light of changing circumstances. For example, a company aiming for market expansion might need to adjust its strategy due to regulatory changes in a new market. Being open to reevaluating and modifying strategies ensures that the company remains on track towards its goals, even in the face of challenges.

Leadership commitment is vital for successful alignment. Leaders at all levels must champion the company's goals and the strategies designed to achieve them. They set the tone for the rest of the organization, demonstrating through their actions and decisions the importance of alignment. This commitment involves not only strategic oversight but also active engagement in the implementation process. Leaders should regularly communicate progress, celebrate successes, and address challenges, reinforcing the strategic direction and keeping the team motivated.

Aligning strategies with company goals also requires a culture of collaboration and teamwork. Achieving strategic goals is rarely the result of individual efforts; it requires the collective effort of the entire organization. Encouraging collaboration across departments and functions can break down silos and foster a more integrated approach to achieving goals. For example, a strategy to improve customer satisfaction might involve input and cooperation from the customer service, product development, and marketing teams. By working together, these teams can ensure that their efforts are complementary and that they are collectively moving towards the same objective.

Moreover, aligning strategies with company goals involves continuous learning and improvement. The business landscape is ever-evolving, and companies must be committed to learning from their experiences and refining their strategies accordingly. This can involve analyzing past performance, seeking feedback from customers and employees, and staying abreast of industry trends and best practices. For instance, after a product launch, a company might conduct a post-mortem analysis to understand what went well and what could be improved, using these insights to enhance future strategies.

Technology and data analytics can greatly aid in the alignment process. Advanced analytics tools can provide real-time insights into performance, helping companies track progress towards their goals and make data-driven decisions. For example, a company might use customer analytics to understand purchasing patterns and preferences, informing its marketing and product development strategies. Technology can also facilitate communication and collaboration, with tools such as project management software and collaborative platforms enabling more efficient and effective strategy implementation.

Finally, aligning strategies with company goals requires a long-term perspective and perseverance. Achieving strategic goals often takes time and sustained effort. It is important for companies to remain committed to their goals, even when progress is slow or challenges arise. This long-term commitment involves regularly revisiting and reaffirming the company's goals and strategies, staying focused on the bigger picture, and maintaining a positive and resilient mindset. For example, a company aiming for significant market share growth might face initial setbacks, but by staying committed to its strategic plan and continuously refining its approach, it can eventually achieve its goal.

Aligning strategies with company goals is a multifaceted and dynamic process that requires clear communication, meticulous planning, continuous monitoring, flexibility, leadership commitment, collaboration, continuous learning, and a long-term perspective. By ensuring that strategies are aligned with the company's goals, organizations can create a cohesive and focused approach to achieving their objectives, driving sustained success and growth. This alignment not only enhances organizational performance but also fosters a unified and motivated workforce, ultimately leading to better business outcomes.

Creating a culture that supports strategic alignment is crucial for sustaining this alignment over time. Organizational culture encompasses the values, beliefs, and behaviors that shape how work gets done within a company. When a culture is aligned with strategic goals, it acts as an invisible hand guiding employee actions and decisions in a way that supports these goals.

Chapter 2

Market Analysis and Competitive Research

Conducting Market Research

Market research is an indispensable tool for businesses aiming to make informed decisions, understand their customers, and stay ahead of competitors. As a beginner, understanding how to conduct effective market research can be the difference between success and failure in your entrepreneurial journey. This chapter delves into the essentials of market research, providing practical and actionable advice to help you gather and analyze data that will guide your business strategies.

Market research begins with defining your goals. What do you want to learn? Are you trying to understand customer preferences, assess the viability of a new product, or analyze competitors? Clear research objectives will guide your entire process, ensuring you collect relevant data. For instance, if you're launching a new health drink, your goal might be to understand consumer attitudes towards health beverages and identify potential market segments.

Once your goals are set, the next step is to choose the right research method. Market research can be broadly categorized into primary and secondary research. Primary research involves collecting new data directly from sources, while secondary research relies on existing data. Primary research methods include surveys, interviews, focus groups, and observations, each offering unique insights.

Surveys are one of the most common primary research tools. They can be distributed online, via email, or even in person. When designing a survey, ensure your questions are clear and concise. Avoid leading questions that could bias the responses. For example, instead of asking, "Do you prefer our amazing new health drink?", you might ask, "How often do you consume health drinks?" and "What factors influence your choice of health drinks?" Surveys can provide quantitative data that is useful for statistical analysis.

Interviews, on the other hand, offer qualitative insights. Conducting one-on-one interviews allows for deeper exploration of individual perceptions and experiences. When conducting interviews, prepare open-ended questions that encourage detailed responses. For instance, asking "Can you describe a recent experience you had with a health drink?" can elicit valuable stories and feedback that might not emerge from a survey.

Focus groups gather a small group of people to discuss a topic in depth. This method can reveal diverse perspectives and spark ideas that you might not have considered. However, focus groups require skilled moderation to ensure that all participants feel comfortable sharing their views and that the discussion stays on track.

Observational research involves watching how people interact with products or services in real-world settings. This method can uncover behaviors and preferences that participants might not consciously articulate. For example, observing shoppers in a supermarket can reveal how they make purchasing decisions about health drinks.

Secondary research involves analyzing existing data, such as industry reports, academic studies, and market analysis by other organizations. This method is often less expensive and quicker than primary research. Sources for secondary research include government publications, industry associations, academic journals, and commercial research firms. For example, analyzing market reports on the beverage industry can provide insights into trends, consumer behaviors, and competitive landscapes.

Data collection is only the beginning. The next crucial step is data analysis. Analyzing quantitative data from surveys involves statistical techniques to identify patterns and trends. Software tools like Excel, SPSS, or specialized survey analysis platforms can help you crunch numbers and visualize data. For example, you might use a bar chart to compare the popularity of different health drink flavors among surveyed consumers.

Qualitative data from interviews and focus groups require different analysis techniques. Thematic analysis involves identifying recurring themes and patterns in the responses. This process can be time-consuming but is essential for uncovering deeper insights. For instance, if multiple interviewees mention concerns about the sugar content in health drinks, this could indicate a potential area for product development or marketing emphasis.

Once you've analyzed your data, it's time to interpret the results and draw conclusions. This step involves linking your findings back to your original research goals. For example, if your survey reveals that a significant portion of your target market prefers natural ingredients in health drinks, you might decide to highlight this feature in your marketing strategy or product formulation.

Effective market research doesn't stop at data collection and analysis; it extends to making informed decisions and taking action based on your findings. For instance, if your research indicates a growing demand for low-calorie health drinks, you might prioritize developing a new product line that caters to this preference. Similarly, if competitor analysis reveals a gap in the market for organic health drinks, you could explore opportunities in this niche.

It's also important to communicate your findings effectively within your organization. Creating a comprehensive market research report can help you share insights with stakeholders, guiding strategic decisions. Your report should include an executive summary, research objectives, methodology, findings, conclusions, and recommendations. Visuals such as charts, graphs, and infographics can make your data more accessible and engaging.

Beyond the initial research phase, continuous market research is vital for staying responsive to changes in the market. Consumer preferences, competitive landscapes, and industry trends are constantly evolving. Regularly updating your market research ensures that your business strategies remain relevant and effective. For instance, conducting annual surveys or quarterly focus groups can help you stay attuned to your customers' needs and adapt accordingly.

Moreover, leveraging digital tools and platforms can enhance your market research efforts. Online survey tools like SurveyMonkey or Google Forms simplify the process of designing and distributing surveys. Social media platforms offer valuable data on consumer behavior and preferences. Analytics tools like Google Analytics can provide insights into website traffic and user behavior, informing your digital marketing strategies.

Ethical considerations are paramount in market research. Ensuring the privacy and confidentiality of your participants is crucial. Obtain informed consent from participants, explaining the purpose of the research and how their data will be used. Avoid deceptive practices and ensure that your research complies with relevant regulations and standards.

In addition to traditional methods, innovative approaches can enrich your market research. For example, ethnographic research involves immersing yourself in the environment of your target market to gain a deeper understanding of their lives and behaviors. This method can uncover rich, contextual insights that other methods might miss. If you're developing health drinks, spending time in fitness centers or health food stores and observing interactions can provide valuable firsthand insights.

Another innovative method is using online communities and panels. These groups consist of pre-recruited participants who agree to take part in ongoing research activities. Online panels can provide quick feedback on new product ideas, marketing campaigns, or customer experiences. This approach offers the advantage of rapid data collection and the ability to track changes in opinions over time.

Finally, always be prepared to adapt your market research strategies as needed. The business environment is dynamic, and what worked yesterday might not be effective today. Stay open to new methods, tools, and sources of data. For example, the rise of big data and machine learning offers new opportunities for market analysis, providing deeper and more accurate insights.

Conducting market research is a multifaceted process that involves setting clear objectives, choosing appropriate methods, collecting and analyzing data, and making informed decisions based on your findings. By mastering these steps, you can gain a competitive edge, understand your customers better, and make strategic decisions that drive your business forward. Remember, market research is not a one-time task but an ongoing effort to stay connected with your market and responsive to its needs.

Investing in continuous market research also helps you build a resilient business strategy that can adapt to unexpected changes in the market landscape. For instance, economic shifts, technological advancements, or sudden changes in consumer behavior can significantly impact your business. By maintaining a regular market research routine, you can anticipate these changes and pivot your strategies accordingly.

Identifying Market Trends

Identifying market trends is a critical skill for any business, whether you're launching a startup or steering an established company. Trends provide insights into the future direction of the market, helping you to anticipate changes, adapt strategies, and seize opportunities before your competitors do. Understanding these patterns can significantly influence product development, marketing strategies, and overall business planning.

First, to identify market trends, it's essential to immerse yourself in industry news and reports. Subscribe to industry publications, follow thought leaders on social media, and attend relevant conferences and webinars. These sources provide a wealth of information about emerging technologies, shifting consumer behaviors, and regulatory changes. For instance, reading a comprehensive market analysis report might reveal a growing interest in sustainable products, prompting you to consider eco-friendly initiatives for your business.

Another effective way to spot trends is by analyzing consumer behavior. This can be done through various data collection methods, such as surveys, focus groups, and social media monitoring. Pay attention to what consumers are saying about your products and services, as well as those of your competitors. Are there recurring themes in their feedback? For example, if you notice an increasing number of customers expressing a desire for fast and free shipping, this could indicate a broader trend towards higher expectations for convenience in e-commerce.

Consumer data from your own business operations can also be a rich source of trend information. Analyzing sales data, website analytics, and customer service interactions can uncover patterns in buying behavior. For example, tracking which products are selling well and identifying seasonal spikes in demand can help you forecast future trends. If you run an online apparel store and notice a significant uptick in sales of athleisure wear, it might be indicative of a broader lifestyle shift towards casual and comfortable clothing.

Competitor analysis is another crucial aspect of trend identification. By keeping a close eye on your competitors, you can gain insights into their strategic moves and market positioning. Regularly review their marketing campaigns, product launches, and public statements. For example, if multiple competitors start offering subscription-box services, it might suggest a growing trend towards personalized and convenient shopping experiences. Understanding these moves allows you to stay competitive and potentially innovate in response.

Technology is often a driving force behind market trends. Advancements in technology can create entirely new markets or transform existing ones. For instance, the rise of smartphones and mobile internet access has revolutionized industries ranging from retail to entertainment. Staying updated on technological developments and considering how they might impact your industry is essential. For example, the increasing adoption of artificial intelligence in customer service could prompt you to explore AI-driven chatbots to enhance your customer support.

Economic indicators also provide valuable insights into market trends. Factors such as employment rates, consumer confidence, and inflation can influence consumer spending patterns and business investments. Keeping an eye on economic reports and understanding their implications can help you anticipate market shifts. For instance, during economic downturns, consumers might prioritize essential goods over luxury items, which could impact your product offerings and marketing strategies.

Social and cultural shifts play a significant role in shaping market trends. Changes in demographics, lifestyles, and societal values can drive new consumer behaviors and preferences. For example, the increasing awareness of health and wellness has led to a surge in demand for organic foods and fitness products. Similarly, the growing focus on environmental sustainability has influenced many industries to adopt greener practices. Staying attuned to these social and cultural dynamics can help you align your business strategies with evolving consumer values.

Leveraging data analytics tools can greatly enhance your ability to identify and analyze market trends. Advanced analytics platforms can process vast amounts of data quickly, revealing patterns and insights that might not be apparent through manual analysis. For instance, predictive analytics can help forecast future trends based on historical data, enabling you to make proactive decisions. If you're running an online business, tools like Google Analytics can provide detailed insights into customer behavior, helping you identify emerging trends and adjust your strategies accordingly.

Networking with industry peers and participating in professional associations can also provide valuable trend insights. Engaging in discussions with other professionals can offer different perspectives and ideas that you might not have considered. Joining industry groups on LinkedIn, participating in forums, and attending local business events can facilitate these interactions. For instance, a casual conversation with a fellow entrepreneur at a conference could reveal an emerging trend that hasn't yet hit mainstream media.

Case studies and success stories from other businesses can serve as a source of inspiration and learning. Analyzing how other companies have successfully identified and capitalized on market trends can provide practical insights and strategies. For example, studying how a leading retailer adapted to the rise of e-commerce by investing in a robust online presence and logistics network can offer valuable lessons for your own business.

It's also important to recognize that not all trends will be relevant to your business. Filtering out the noise and focusing on trends that align with your core competencies and market positioning is crucial. For example, while the trend towards virtual reality might be exciting, it may not be pertinent if your business operates in a completely different industry. Prioritize trends that have a direct impact on your target audience and business objectives.

Adapting to identified trends requires a flexible and agile approach. Being open to change and willing to experiment with new ideas can help you stay ahead of the curve. For instance, if you identify a trend towards personalized customer experiences, you might experiment with personalized email marketing campaigns or customized product recommendations. These small-scale experiments can provide valuable insights and inform larger strategic decisions.

Finally, regularly reviewing and updating your understanding of market trends is essential. The business environment is dynamic, and trends can evolve rapidly. Establishing a routine for trend analysis, such as quarterly reviews, can help ensure that your strategies remain relevant and effective. Involving your team in these reviews can also foster a culture of continuous learning and innovation within your organization.

Identifying market trends is a multifaceted process that involves staying informed, analyzing data, and being open to change. By immersing yourself in industry news, understanding consumer behavior, monitoring competitors, leveraging technology, and engaging with peers, you can gain valuable insights into emerging trends. These insights enable you to anticipate changes, adapt your strategies, and seize opportunities, ultimately driving the success and growth of your business. Embracing a proactive and agile approach to trend identification ensures that you stay ahead in a constantly evolving market landscape.

In addition to the strategies already discussed, another powerful tool for identifying market trends is leveraging social listening. Social listening involves monitoring social media platforms for mentions of your brand, products, industry keywords, and competitors. This real-time feedback can provide immediate insights into what consumers are talking about, their preferences, and emerging trends. Tools like Hootsuite, Brandwatch, and Sprout Social can help you track and analyze these conversations. For example, if you notice a surge in discussions about plant-based diets on Twitter and Instagram, this could signal a growing trend towards vegan and vegetarian food options that your business could capitalize on.

Analyzing Competitors

Understanding your competitors is a fundamental aspect of running a successful business. By analyzing competitors, you can uncover valuable insights into market positioning, customer preferences, and potential gaps in the market. This knowledge can inform your strategic decisions, helping you to differentiate your offerings and stay ahead in the competitive landscape.

The first step in analyzing competitors is identifying who they are. Competitors can be direct, offering similar products or services to the same target audience, or indirect, providing alternative solutions that meet the same customer needs. Start by listing your direct competitors—those businesses that offer products or services almost identical to yours. Then, expand this list to include indirect competitors that may not be immediately obvious but still impact your market. For example, a local bakery might see other bakeries as direct competitors, while supermarkets with bakery sections represent indirect competition.

Once you have identified your competitors, gather information about them. This can be done through various methods, including online research, mystery shopping, and leveraging customer feedback. Visit competitors' websites and social media profiles to understand their brand messaging, product range, pricing, and customer engagement strategies. Pay attention to customer reviews and ratings on platforms like Yelp, Google Reviews, and social media comments. These reviews can provide insights into what customers like or dislike about your competitors, highlighting areas where you can improve your own offerings.

Mystery shopping involves experiencing your competitors' products or services firsthand. This could mean purchasing a product, using a service, or visiting a physical store. Take note of the entire customer experience, from the ease of navigation on their website to the quality of customer service and the final product. This firsthand perspective can reveal strengths and weaknesses in your competitors' operations, offering you a clearer understanding of where you can gain a competitive edge.

Analyzing competitors' marketing strategies is another crucial aspect. Look at their advertising campaigns, social media activities, content marketing efforts, and promotions. What channels are they using to reach their audience? How do they position their brand? For instance, if a competitor is heavily investing in influencer marketing and seeing significant engagement, it might be worth considering a similar approach. Additionally, examine their SEO strategies by identifying the keywords they rank for and the type of content they produce. Tools like SEMrush or Ahrefs can provide detailed insights into competitors' online visibility and traffic sources.

Understanding competitors' pricing strategies is essential for positioning your own products or services effectively. Compare their prices with yours and evaluate the perceived value they offer. Are they competing on price, offering significant discounts and promotions, or are they positioning themselves as premium brands with higher price points? Analyzing their pricing can help you determine whether you need to adjust your prices to remain competitive or emphasize the unique value your offerings provide.

Product analysis is another critical component. Evaluate the features, benefits, and overall quality of your competitors' products or services. What makes their offerings stand out? Are there any features that customers particularly appreciate or criticize? Identifying these aspects can guide your product development efforts, helping you to enhance your offerings or introduce new features that address unmet needs in the market. For example, if a competitor's product is praised for its user-friendly interface, you might consider improving the usability of your own product to match or exceed customer expectations.

Examining competitors' distribution and sales channels can provide insights into how they reach their customers and whether there are opportunities for you to expand your reach. Are they selling directly through their website, using third-party marketplaces like Amazon, or partnering with physical retailers? Understanding their distribution strategy can help you identify new channels to explore or areas where you can improve your reach and convenience for customers.

Customer service is a crucial area where businesses can differentiate themselves. Analyze how your competitors handle customer inquiries, complaints, and support. Are they responsive and helpful? Do they offer multiple channels for customer support, such as live chat, email, and phone support? High-quality customer service can be a significant competitive advantage, so identifying gaps in your competitors' customer service can help you enhance your own support offerings.

It's also important to understand the financial health and business performance of your competitors. Public companies often release financial statements and annual reports that provide insights into their revenue, profitability, and growth strategies. For private companies, you might rely on industry reports, market research, and any available financial data. Understanding their financial position can help you gauge their ability to invest in new initiatives, withstand economic downturns, and compete in the long term.

Competitors' strategic partnerships and alliances can also offer valuable insights. Identify any collaborations they have with other businesses, organizations, or influencers. These partnerships can enhance their market presence, credibility, and customer reach. For example, if a competitor has partnered with a well-known brand to co-create a product or service, it might be worth exploring similar partnership opportunities to boost your own brand's visibility and appeal.

Monitoring competitors over time is crucial for staying updated on their strategies and market position. Set up alerts for news and updates related to your competitors using tools like Google Alerts. Regularly review their website, social media, and marketing campaigns to identify any changes or new initiatives. This ongoing monitoring ensures that you remain aware of any shifts in their strategy that could impact your business.

Finally, conducting a SWOT analysis (Strengths, Weaknesses, Opportunities, and Threats) for your competitors can provide a comprehensive overview of their position in the market. Identify their strengths and weaknesses relative to your own business, and look for opportunities where you can capitalize on their weaknesses or market gaps. Additionally, consider any threats they pose to your business and develop strategies to mitigate these risks.

Analyzing competitors is a multifaceted process that involves gathering and interpreting a wide range of information. By identifying your competitors, researching their operations, marketing strategies, pricing, products, distribution channels, customer service, financial health, and strategic partnerships, you can gain a thorough understanding of the competitive landscape. This knowledge enables you to make informed decisions, differentiate your offerings, and strategically position your business for success. Continuously monitoring competitors and adapting to changes in the market ensures that you remain competitive and responsive to emerging trends and challenges.

SWOT Analysis

One often overlooked aspect of analyzing competitors is understanding their culture and organizational structure. The way a company is run internally can have a significant impact on its external performance. Investigate the leadership styles, company values, and employee satisfaction levels of your competitors. Websites like Glassdoor and LinkedIn can provide insights into employee reviews and company culture. If a competitor is known for fostering a positive work environment and has high employee retention, this might reflect in their customer service and overall business performance. Conversely, a company with high turnover and negative employee feedback might struggle with consistency and customer satisfaction.

Leveraging Market Insights

Market insights are the backbone of any strategic business decision. Leveraging these insights effectively can mean the difference between success and stagnation. Market insights provide a comprehensive understanding of your industry, your customers, and the trends that shape the market landscape. They are derived from data analysis, customer feedback, competitive intelligence, and industry reports. By harnessing this information, businesses can make informed decisions, anticipate market shifts, and tailor their strategies to meet evolving demands.

The first step in leveraging market insights is gathering relevant data. Data can come from various sources, including customer surveys, social media analytics, sales reports, and third-party market research. Each source offers a unique perspective, contributing to a holistic view of the market. For example, customer surveys can reveal preferences and pain points, while social media analytics can show real-time trends and consumer sentiment. Sales reports provide concrete data on what products or services are performing well, and third-party research can offer macro-level insights into industry trends.

Once the data is collected, the next step is analysis. This involves transforming raw data into meaningful insights. Statistical tools and software can help identify patterns and trends that might not be immediately obvious. For instance, a spike in sales during a particular season or a dip in customer satisfaction following a product change are patterns that can guide strategic decisions. Analyzing data also involves segmentation—breaking down the data into specific groups to understand different customer behaviors. For instance, segmenting your customer base by age, location, or purchasing behavior can reveal targeted insights that help tailor your marketing strategies.

A practical example of leveraging market insights is seen in the retail industry. Consider a clothing retailer facing declining sales. By analyzing sales data, customer feedback, and market trends, the retailer might discover that younger customers prefer sustainable fashion. This insight can lead to a strategic shift towards eco-friendly products, revamped marketing campaigns highlighting sustainability, and even partnerships with sustainable brands. The retailer's ability to adapt based on market insights can help reverse declining sales and attract a new customer base.

Another crucial aspect of leveraging market insights is staying ahead of trends. Market trends can significantly impact your business, and being proactive rather than reactive can provide a competitive edge. This means continuously monitoring industry news, attending trade shows, and networking with industry experts. For example, a tech company that identifies an emerging trend in artificial intelligence can start investing in relevant technologies and talent before the trend becomes mainstream. This foresight can position the company as a leader in the industry, ready to capitalize on new opportunities as they arise.

Customer insights are a subset of market insights that deserve special attention. Understanding your customers deeply—what they need, what they value, and how they behave—can drive product development, marketing, and customer service strategies. Tools like customer relationship management (CRM) systems can track customer interactions and purchase history, providing valuable data for analysis. By identifying patterns in customer behavior, businesses can personalize their approaches, leading to higher satisfaction and loyalty. For instance, an e-commerce platform might use purchase history data to recommend products tailored to individual customers, enhancing the shopping experience and increasing sales.

Competitor analysis is another vital component. Understanding your competitors' strategies, strengths, and weaknesses can provide insights into your own positioning and opportunities. This involves not just looking at their product offerings but also their marketing strategies, customer experiences, and market perceptions. For example, if a competitor is successfully engaging customers through a new social media platform, it might be worth exploring similar strategies. Conversely, identifying gaps or weaknesses in competitors' offerings can highlight areas where your business can excel.

Market insights also play a crucial role in risk management. By understanding market dynamics and potential disruptions, businesses can develop contingency plans to mitigate risks. This includes economic shifts, regulatory changes, and technological advancements. For instance, a financial services firm might use market insights to anticipate regulatory changes and adjust their compliance strategies accordingly. Similarly, a manufacturing company might monitor supply chain trends to identify potential disruptions and develop alternative sourcing strategies.

Incorporating market insights into strategic planning ensures that your business decisions are data-driven and forward-looking. This involves setting up regular review processes where market data is analyzed, and insights are integrated into strategic discussions. For example, quarterly business reviews might include a segment dedicated to market insights, where key findings are presented and discussed. This ensures that all strategic decisions are grounded in current market realities and future projections.

Leveraging market insights also requires a culture of data-driven decision-making within the organization. This means fostering an environment where data is valued, and employees are trained to interpret and use it effectively. Providing access to data and analytical tools across departments can empower teams to make informed decisions. For example, marketing teams can use customer insights to craft targeted campaigns, while product development teams can use market trends to innovate new features. Encouraging collaboration across departments ensures that insights are shared and integrated into all aspects of the business.

Technology plays a significant role in harnessing market insights. Advanced analytics, machine learning, and artificial intelligence can process vast amounts of data quickly and accurately, uncovering insights that might be missed by manual analysis. Investing in the right technology infrastructure is crucial for effective data analysis and insight generation. For instance, a cloud-based analytics platform can provide real-time data access and powerful analytical capabilities, enabling businesses to react swiftly to market changes.

Finally, it's essential to act on the insights gained. Collecting and analyzing data is only valuable if it leads to actionable strategies. This means translating insights into concrete actions, whether it's adjusting your product line, shifting marketing strategies, or exploring new markets. For example, if market insights reveal a growing demand for a particular product feature, the development team should prioritize its implementation. Similarly, if customer feedback highlights dissatisfaction with a service aspect, immediate steps should be taken to address and improve it.

In conclusion, leveraging market insights is a dynamic and ongoing process that requires diligence, strategic thinking, and a willingness to adapt. By gathering comprehensive data, analyzing it effectively, and translating insights into actionable strategies, businesses can make informed decisions that drive growth and innovation. Staying attuned to market trends, understanding customer needs, and continuously monitoring competitors ensures that your business remains competitive and responsive to changing market dynamics. This proactive approach not only enhances current performance but also positions your business for long-term success in an ever-evolving marketplace.

Market insights should also inform your approach to customer communication and engagement. Knowing what your customers value and how they prefer to interact with your brand allows you to tailor your messaging and channels accordingly. For instance, if data indicates that your target demographic prefers concise updates via social media rather than lengthy email newsletters, you should adjust your communication strategy to align with these preferences. By doing so, you not only increase engagement but also build stronger relationships with your customers.

Chapter 3

Strategic Planning Fundamentals

Creating a Strategic Plan

Creating a strategic plan is essential for any organization aiming to achieve long-term success. A strategic plan serves as a roadmap, guiding the organization through its goals and objectives while navigating the complexities and uncertainties of the market. It aligns the entire organization towards common objectives, ensuring that every department and team member understands their role in achieving the overarching vision.

To begin crafting a strategic plan, it's crucial to start with a clear vision and mission statement. The vision statement outlines what the organization aspires to become in the future, while the mission statement defines the organization's purpose and primary objectives. These statements provide a foundation for all strategic planning activities, ensuring that every goal and action aligns with the core values and long-term aspirations of the organization. For example, a healthcare company might have a vision to be the leading provider of innovative health solutions and a mission to improve patient outcomes through cutting-edge technology and compassionate care.

The next step is conducting a thorough situational analysis, often referred to as a SWOT analysis. This involves identifying the organization's internal strengths and weaknesses, as well as external opportunities and threats. Strengths might include a strong brand reputation, proprietary technology, or a skilled workforce. Weaknesses could be outdated technology, limited market presence, or financial constraints. Opportunities might come from emerging markets, technological advancements, or shifting consumer behavior. Threats could include economic downturns, regulatory changes, or new competitors entering the market. By understanding these factors, the organization can leverage its strengths, address its weaknesses, capitalize on opportunities, and mitigate potential threats.

Setting clear, measurable goals is the cornerstone of a strategic plan. Goals should be specific, measurable, achievable, relevant, and time-bound (SMART). For instance, instead of setting a vague goal like "increase sales," a SMART goal would be "increase sales by 15% within the next 12 months through expanding into new markets and enhancing online marketing efforts." This level of specificity ensures that progress can be tracked, and success can be quantified.

Once goals are established, developing actionable strategies to achieve them is the next step. Strategies outline the approach the organization will take to reach its goals. They should be detailed and consider various aspects such as market positioning, product development, marketing campaigns, and operational improvements. For example, if one of the goals is to expand into new markets, the strategy might involve conducting market research to identify viable regions, forming partnerships with local distributors, and tailoring marketing campaigns to the preferences of the new audience.

Resource allocation is a critical component of strategic planning. This involves determining the financial, human, and technological resources required to execute the strategies. Effective resource allocation ensures that the organization has the necessary tools and capabilities to achieve its goals without overextending itself. For instance, if expanding into new markets requires additional sales personnel, the strategic plan should outline the hiring process, training programs, and budget allocations needed to support this expansion.

Implementing the strategic plan requires a detailed action plan. This plan should break down each strategy into specific tasks, assign responsibilities, and set deadlines. For example, if the strategy is to enhance online marketing efforts, the action plan might include tasks such as hiring a digital marketing specialist, redesigning the website, launching targeted advertising campaigns, and monitoring performance metrics. Assigning clear responsibilities ensures accountability and helps track progress towards the goals.

Communication is key to successful implementation. The strategic plan should be communicated effectively throughout the organization, ensuring that everyone understands their role and how their efforts contribute to the overall objectives. Regular updates and progress reports keep the team informed and motivated. For instance, monthly meetings could be held to review progress, address challenges, and make necessary adjustments to the plan.

Monitoring and evaluating the progress of the strategic plan is essential. This involves regularly reviewing key performance indicators (KPIs) to assess whether the organization is on track to achieve its goals. KPIs might include metrics such as sales growth, market share, customer satisfaction, and operational efficiency. If the organization is not meeting its targets, it's important to analyze the reasons and make necessary adjustments. This could involve reallocating resources, revising strategies, or even redefining goals if market conditions have changed significantly.

Flexibility is crucial in strategic planning. The business environment is constantly evolving, and organizations must be prepared to adapt their plans as needed. This means being open to new information, willing to pivot strategies, and continuously learning from both successes and failures. For example, if a competitor launches a disruptive new product, the organization might need to accelerate its own product development timeline or adjust its marketing strategies to maintain its competitive edge.

Engaging stakeholders throughout the strategic planning process can enhance the plan's effectiveness. This includes involving employees, customers, suppliers, and investors in discussions and gathering their insights. For instance, employees on the front lines can provide valuable feedback on operational challenges and customer preferences, while customers can offer insights into their needs and expectations. Engaging stakeholders not only enriches the planning process with diverse perspectives but also fosters a sense of ownership and commitment to the plan's success.

Regularly revisiting and updating the strategic plan ensures that it remains relevant and effective. This involves conducting periodic reviews to assess progress, evaluate market conditions, and incorporate new information. For example, an annual review might involve revisiting the SWOT analysis, adjusting goals based on the previous year's performance, and updating strategies to reflect changes in the competitive landscape. Continuous improvement ensures that the strategic plan evolves with the organization and the market, maintaining its effectiveness over time.

Celebrating milestones and successes along the way can boost morale and reinforce the importance of the strategic plan. Recognizing and rewarding achievements, whether large or small, keeps the team motivated and focused on the long-term vision. For instance, if a goal to increase sales by 15% is achieved, celebrating this success with the team not only acknowledges their hard work but also reinforces the value of strategic planning.

Ultimately, creating a strategic plan is an ongoing process that requires dedication, collaboration, and adaptability. It's not a document that is created once and then forgotten, but a living framework that guides the organization towards its goals. By starting with a clear vision and mission, conducting a thorough situational analysis, setting SMART goals, developing actionable strategies, allocating resources effectively, and continuously monitoring progress, organizations can navigate the complexities of the market and achieve long-term success.

In conclusion, strategic planning is an essential practice for any organization aiming to thrive in a competitive and dynamic market. It provides a structured approach to setting goals, developing strategies, and allocating resources, ensuring that every action taken is aligned with the organization's vision and mission. By fostering a culture of data-driven decision-making, continuous improvement, and stakeholder engagement, organizations can create strategic plans that not only guide them towards their objectives but also equip them to adapt and succeed in an ever-changing business environment.

Maintaining alignment between the strategic plan and the organization's day-to-day operations is crucial for sustained success. This involves integrating the strategic plan into the organization's culture and ensuring that it influences decision-making at all levels. Leaders play a pivotal role in this integration, as they must embody the strategic vision and communicate its importance consistently. For instance, in team meetings, leaders can reference the strategic goals when discussing projects and performance, creating a clear link between daily tasks and the broader objectives.

Resource Allocation

Effective resource allocation is the backbone of any successful organization. It involves the strategic distribution of financial, human, and material resources to maximize efficiency and achieve organizational goals. Without proper resource allocation, even the most well-thought-out strategic plans can falter. To allocate resources effectively, it's essential to understand the organization's priorities, capabilities, and constraints. This process requires a balance between meeting immediate needs and investing in long-term growth.

The first step in resource allocation is to thoroughly assess the organization's current resources. This includes a detailed inventory of financial assets, workforce skills, technological tools, and physical infrastructure. Understanding these resources helps in identifying gaps and surpluses, ensuring that the allocation is based on accurate data. For example, a company looking to expand its market presence might first assess its marketing budget, the expertise of its marketing team, and the effectiveness of its current marketing tools. This assessment provides a clear picture of what is available and what additional resources are needed.

Once the current resources are assessed, the next step is to align them with the organization's strategic goals. This involves prioritizing initiatives that are most critical to achieving these goals. For instance, if a company's primary objective is to innovate its product line, resources should be directed towards research and development. This might mean reallocating funds from less critical areas or temporarily scaling back on certain operations to free up resources. Prioritization ensures that the most important projects receive the necessary support and attention.

Budgeting plays a crucial role in resource allocation. Developing a detailed budget that outlines expected revenues and expenditures helps in managing financial resources effectively. This budget should be flexible enough to accommodate unexpected changes while maintaining a focus on strategic priorities. For example, an organization might set aside a contingency fund to address unforeseen expenses without compromising its strategic initiatives. Regularly reviewing and adjusting the budget ensures that the allocation of financial resources remains aligned with the organization's goals. resources are equally important in the allocation process. Ensuring that the right people are in the right roles is essential for maximizing productivity and achieving strategic objectives. This might involve hiring new talent, providing additional training to existing employees, or redistributing tasks to better align with individual strengths and organizational needs. For instance, if a company is launching a new product, it might need to hire specialized marketing professionals or provide current employees with training in new marketing techniques. Effective human resource allocation not only boosts performance but also enhances employee satisfaction and retention.

Technology and tools are another critical aspect of resource allocation. Investing in the right technology can significantly enhance efficiency and productivity. This might involve upgrading outdated systems, implementing new software solutions, or investing in cutting-edge technology that provides a competitive advantage. For example, a company looking to improve its customer service might invest in a new customer relationship management (CRM) system that streamlines interactions and provides valuable insights into customer preferences. Regularly evaluating and updating technological resources ensures that the organization remains competitive and capable of meeting its strategic goals.

Physical resources, such as office space, equipment, and inventory, also require careful allocation. Ensuring that these resources are used efficiently can reduce costs and improve operational effectiveness. This might involve optimizing the use of office space through flexible working arrangements, investing in energy-efficient equipment, or managing inventory to reduce waste and improve supply chain efficiency. For instance, a manufacturing company might implement lean production techniques to minimize waste and maximize the use of raw materials. Effective management of physical resources contributes to the overall efficiency and sustainability of the organization.

Communication is key to successful resource allocation. Ensuring that all stakeholders understand the allocation decisions and their rationale helps in gaining support and minimizing resistance. This can be achieved through regular updates, transparent decision-making processes, and involving key stakeholders in the allocation discussions. For example, if a company decides to reallocate resources from one department to another, explaining the strategic importance of this decision and how it benefits the organization as a whole can foster understanding and cooperation. Clear communication ensures that everyone is aligned with the organization's priorities and working towards common goals.

Monitoring and evaluating the effectiveness of resource allocation is crucial for continuous improvement. This involves setting clear metrics for success and regularly reviewing performance against these metrics. For instance, if resources are allocated to a new marketing campaign, measuring its impact on sales, brand awareness, and customer engagement can provide valuable insights into its effectiveness. If the results fall short of expectations, adjustments can be made to improve future allocations. Continuous monitoring and evaluation ensure that resources are used efficiently and effectively, contributing to the organization's long-term success.

Flexibility is essential in resource allocation. The business environment is dynamic, and organizations must be able to adapt to changes quickly. This might involve reallocating resources in response to market shifts, technological advancements, or unexpected challenges. For example, during an economic downturn, an organization might need to shift resources from growth initiatives to cost-cutting measures. Being flexible and responsive ensures that the organization can navigate uncertainties and remain resilient in the face of change.

Scenario planning is a valuable tool in resource allocation. By considering different possible future scenarios, organizations can develop contingency plans and allocate resources accordingly. This proactive approach helps in anticipating potential challenges and opportunities, ensuring that the organization is prepared for various outcomes. For instance, a company might develop scenarios for different economic conditions and allocate resources to ensure stability and growth under each scenario. Scenario planning enhances strategic agility and ensures that resources are allocated in a way that supports long-term resilience.

Resource allocation is not a one-time activity but an ongoing process that requires continuous attention and adjustment. Regularly revisiting the allocation decisions and making necessary adjustments ensures that resources remain aligned with the organization's evolving goals and priorities. This might involve conducting quarterly reviews, setting up a resource allocation committee, or using advanced analytics to track resource utilization. An iterative approach to resource allocation ensures that the organization remains agile, efficient, and focused on achieving its strategic objectives.

In conclusion, effective resource allocation is fundamental to the success of any organization. By thoroughly assessing current resources, aligning them with strategic goals, prioritizing initiatives, and maintaining flexibility, organizations can ensure that their resources are used efficiently and effectively. Clear communication, continuous monitoring, and scenario planning further enhance the allocation process, contributing to long-term resilience and success. As the business environment continues to evolve, a proactive and dynamic approach to resource allocation will enable organizations to navigate challenges and seize opportunities, driving sustainable growth and achievement of their strategic objectives.

Additionally, the integration of a systematic approach to resource allocation can significantly enhance organizational effectiveness. One such approach is the use of resource allocation frameworks or models. These frameworks provide a structured method for decision-making, ensuring that all factors are considered, and resources are allocated optimally. For instance, the Balanced Scorecard approach integrates financial and non-financial performance measures to provide a comprehensive view of organizational performance. By aligning resource allocation with the Balanced Scorecard's perspectives—financial, customer, internal processes, and learning and growth—organizations can ensure that resources are supporting balanced and sustainable growth.

Risk Management Strategies

Risk management is an essential component of any organization's strategy, ensuring that potential threats are identified, assessed, and mitigated before they can impact operations. Effective risk management not only protects the organization but also enhances its ability to achieve its objectives and sustain long-term growth. Understanding and implementing comprehensive risk management strategies can make the difference between a thriving business and one that continuously struggles to navigate uncertainties.

To begin with, risk identification is the foundational step in the risk management process. This involves systematically recognizing potential risks that could affect the organization. These risks can be internal, such as operational inefficiencies, or external, like economic downturns or natural disasters. Engaging stakeholders across different levels of the organization during this phase is crucial, as they can provide diverse perspectives and insights. For instance, while senior management might highlight strategic risks, frontline employees might identify operational issues that could escalate if left unaddressed.

Once risks are identified, the next step is risk assessment. This involves evaluating the likelihood of each risk occurring and its potential impact on the organization. Quantitative methods, such as statistical analysis and financial modeling, can be used to assess risks in measurable terms. Qualitative methods, like expert judgment and scenario analysis, provide valuable insights where data might be limited. For example, assessing the risk of a cyber-attack would involve not only analyzing past incidents and potential vulnerabilities but also considering expert opinions on emerging threats.

Following the assessment, risk prioritization helps in focusing on the most critical risks. Not all risks require equal attention; hence, it is essential to prioritize them based on their potential impact and likelihood. Creating a risk matrix can be an effective way to visualize and prioritize risks. This tool plots risks on a grid, with one axis representing the likelihood and the other the impact. High-impact, high-likelihood risks are prioritized for immediate action, while low-impact, low-likelihood risks are monitored periodically. For example, a manufacturing company might prioritize risks related to supply chain disruptions over minor operational inefficiencies.

Mitigation strategies form the core of risk management. These strategies are actions taken to reduce the likelihood of risks occurring or to minimize their impact if they do occur. Mitigation can involve a range of activities, such as implementing new policies, investing in technology, or enhancing employee training. For instance, to mitigate the risk of data breaches, an organization might invest in advanced cybersecurity measures, conduct regular security audits, and train employees on best practices for data protection.

Transferring risk is another effective strategy. This involves shifting the risk to a third party, typically through insurance or outsourcing. By transferring risk, the organization can protect itself from potential losses without bearing the full burden. For example, purchasing property insurance transfers the financial risk of damage due to fire or natural disasters to the insurance company. Similarly, outsourcing IT services to a specialized provider can transfer the risk of technology failures and associated downtime.

Risk avoidance is a strategy where the organization decides not to engage in activities that carry unacceptable levels of risk. This might involve forgoing certain projects, markets, or practices altogether. For instance, a company might decide not to enter a volatile market to avoid the high risk of financial losses. While this strategy can limit opportunities, it ensures that the organization does not expose itself to risks beyond its risk appetite.

Accepting risk, or risk retention, is a strategy where the organization acknowledges the presence of certain risks and decides to deal with them as they arise. This approach is suitable for risks that are minor or where the cost of mitigation exceeds the potential impact. For example, a retail store might accept the risk of minor shoplifting incidents rather than investing heavily in advanced security systems. This strategy requires a clear understanding of the organization's risk tolerance and the ability to respond effectively when risks materialize.

Communication and consultation are vital throughout the risk management process. Keeping all stakeholders informed about risks and the measures being taken to address them fosters a culture of transparency and collaboration. Regular communication ensures that everyone is aware of their roles and responsibilities in managing risks. For instance, monthly risk management meetings can provide a platform for discussing new risks, reviewing mitigation efforts, and making necessary adjustments.

Monitoring and review are ongoing processes that ensure the risk management strategies remain effective. Regularly reviewing risks and the effectiveness of mitigation measures allows the organization to adapt to changing circumstances. This can involve periodic risk assessments, internal audits, and performance reviews. For example, if a new regulation impacts the organization's operations, a review might reveal the need to update compliance measures and allocate additional resources.

Embedding risk management into the organizational culture enhances its effectiveness. This involves integrating risk awareness and management practices into daily operations and decision-making processes. By fostering a risk-aware culture, employees at all levels are encouraged to proactively identify and address risks. Training programs, workshops, and regular communication can help in building this culture. For instance, incorporating risk management training into the onboarding process for new employees ensures that they understand the organization's approach to risk from the outset.

Leveraging technology can significantly enhance risk management efforts. Advanced analytics, artificial intelligence, and machine learning can provide deeper insights into risk patterns and trends, enabling more accurate predictions and timely interventions. For example, predictive analytics can help in identifying potential supply chain disruptions before they occur, allowing the organization to take preemptive action. Implementing risk management software can streamline the process, providing a centralized platform for tracking risks, mitigation efforts, and outcomes.

Collaboration with external partners, such as industry associations, regulatory bodies, and other organizations, can provide valuable insights and resources for managing risks. Sharing information about common risks and best practices enhances collective resilience. For example, participating in industry forums can provide early warnings about emerging risks and opportunities to collaborate on mitigation strategies.

Scenario planning is a proactive approach that involves envisioning different future scenarios and developing strategies to address potential risks. This helps in preparing for uncertainties and ensures that the organization can respond quickly and effectively. For instance, a company might develop scenarios for different economic conditions and outline corresponding risk management strategies. By preparing for various possibilities, the organization enhances its resilience and agility.

In conclusion, effective risk management requires a comprehensive and dynamic approach. By systematically identifying, assessing, and prioritizing risks, organizations can implement targeted mitigation strategies that protect their operations and support their strategic objectives. Embracing a culture of risk awareness, leveraging technology, and collaborating with external partners further enhance risk management efforts. Continuous monitoring and adaptation ensure that the organization remains resilient in the face of changing risks, enabling sustained success and growth.

Ultimately, the effectiveness of risk management lies in its integration into the fabric of the organization. This means that risk management should not be viewed as a standalone function but rather as an integral part of strategic planning and everyday operations. When embedded seamlessly, it empowers the organization to navigate uncertainties with confidence and agility.

Implementing Strategic Initiatives

Implementing strategic initiatives requires careful planning, diligent execution, and continuous evaluation to ensure that organizational goals are met. Strategic initiatives are the specific actions and projects that drive an organization toward its long-term objectives. To successfully implement these initiatives, it is crucial to align them with the overall strategy, secure the necessary resources, and engage all stakeholders throughout the process.

The first step in implementing strategic initiatives is to clearly define the initiative and its objectives. This involves outlining the desired outcomes, the scope of the project, and the key performance indicators (KPIs) that will be used to measure success. For example, if an organization aims to expand its market share by launching a new product line, the strategic initiative would include specific goals such as product development timelines, market research activities, and sales targets. Clearly defined objectives provide a roadmap for the initiative and help ensure that all team members are working towards the same goals.

Once the objectives are set, it is essential to develop a detailed implementation plan. This plan should include timelines, milestones, and responsibilities. Breaking down the initiative into smaller, manageable tasks helps to track progress and maintain momentum. For instance, a company planning to enter a new market might break the initiative into stages such as market analysis, product adaptation, regulatory compliance, and marketing launch. Each stage would have specific milestones and deadlines, ensuring that the initiative progresses systematically and stays on schedule.

Securing the necessary resources is a critical aspect of implementing strategic initiatives. Resources can include financial investments, personnel, technology, and external expertise. It is important to conduct a thorough assessment of the resources required and ensure they are available before beginning the initiative. For example, a tech company developing a new software product would need to allocate budget for research and development, hire skilled developers, and possibly engage with external consultants for specialized knowledge. Ensuring resource availability helps prevent delays and enables smooth execution.

Engaging stakeholders is another vital component of successful implementation. Stakeholders can include employees, customers, suppliers, and investors. Effective communication and involvement of stakeholders create buy-in and support for the initiative. For instance, involving employees in the planning process through workshops or brainstorming sessions can generate valuable insights and foster a sense of ownership. Regular updates and feedback loops with customers and suppliers can also provide critical information that shapes the initiative's direction and increases its chances of success.

Leadership plays a crucial role in guiding the implementation of strategic initiatives. Strong leadership ensures that the initiative remains aligned with the organization's vision and values. Leaders must communicate the importance of the initiative, motivate the team, and address any challenges that arise. For example, a CEO spearheading a digital transformation initiative must articulate the benefits of the transformation, provide support for employees adapting to new technologies, and resolve any resistance or issues promptly. Effective leadership ensures that the initiative stays on course and maintains momentum.

Monitoring progress and making adjustments as needed are essential to the successful implementation of strategic initiatives. Regularly tracking KPIs and milestones allows for early identification of issues and enables timely interventions. For instance, if a marketing campaign is not generating the expected leads, the team can analyze the data, identify the problem, and adjust the strategy accordingly. Continuous monitoring and flexibility in approach ensure that the initiative can adapt to changing circumstances and remain effective.

Celebrating successes and recognizing contributions is important for maintaining morale and motivation throughout the implementation process. Acknowledging milestones and achievements reinforces the value of the initiative and encourages continued effort and commitment. For example, publicly recognizing the hard work of a project team upon reaching a significant milestone can boost morale and foster a positive organizational culture. Celebrations and recognition help sustain enthusiasm and drive for the initiative's success.

Evaluating the outcomes of strategic initiatives is crucial for learning and improvement. After the initiative is completed, a thorough evaluation should be conducted to assess whether the objectives were met and to identify lessons learned. This evaluation provides valuable insights that can inform future initiatives. For example, a post-project review might reveal that certain strategies were particularly effective or that specific challenges need to be addressed differently in the future. Learning from these experiences enhances the organization's ability to implement future initiatives successfully.

One case study that illustrates effective implementation of strategic initiatives is the turnaround of IBM in the 1990s. Faced with declining profits and market share, then-CEO Lou Gerstner implemented a series of strategic initiatives focused on transforming IBM from a hardware-centric company to a service-oriented business. This involved significant changes, including the development of new service offerings, restructuring of the organization, and cultural transformation to embrace customer-centricity. Gerstner's clear vision, effective leadership, and focus on execution enabled IBM to successfully navigate the transformation and regain its competitive edge. This example highlights the importance of aligning initiatives with strategic goals, securing resources, engaging stakeholders, and maintaining strong leadership throughout the process.

On a smaller scale, consider a mid-sized retail company aiming to enhance its online presence. The strategic initiative might include developing an e-commerce platform, optimizing inventory management, and launching targeted digital marketing campaigns. The implementation plan would involve setting up a project team, defining clear milestones such as website launch dates, and allocating budget for technology and marketing spend. Engaging with customers through surveys and feedback sessions would ensure the new platform meets their needs. Regular progress reviews and adjustments based on customer feedback and market trends would keep the initiative on track. Recognizing the efforts of the team upon reaching key milestones, such as the first 1,000 online sales, would boost morale and drive continued success.

In conclusion, implementing strategic initiatives requires a structured approach, from defining clear objectives and developing detailed plans to securing resources and engaging stakeholders. Strong leadership, continuous monitoring, and flexibility are essential to navigate challenges and adapt to changes. Recognizing achievements and learning from experiences further enhance the organization's ability to execute future initiatives successfully. By following these principles, organizations can effectively implement strategic initiatives and achieve their long-term goals, driving growth and innovation.

Strategic initiatives are the engines of transformation and growth within an organization. To illustrate further, let us delve into the example of a healthcare provider aiming to implement a strategic initiative centered on improving patient care through technology integration.

Monitoring and Adjusting Strategies

Monitoring and adjusting strategies are essential processes for ensuring that an organization remains on track to achieve its objectives. A strategy, no matter how well-conceived, is not a static document. It requires constant vigilance and flexibility to respond to internal and external changes. This dynamic approach helps organizations stay competitive and resilient in an ever-evolving market landscape.

Effective monitoring begins with establishing clear metrics and key performance indicators (KPIs) that align with the strategic goals. These metrics provide a quantitative means to assess progress and performance. For instance, if a company aims to increase its market share, relevant KPIs might include sales growth, customer acquisition rates, and market penetration. By regularly reviewing these indicators, an organization can gauge whether it is moving in the right direction or if adjustments are necessary.

Consider a retail company that has set a goal to expand its online presence. The company might track metrics such as website traffic, conversion rates, average order value, and customer retention rates. Regularly analyzing these metrics helps the company understand the effectiveness of its online marketing strategies and identify areas for improvement. For example, if website traffic is high but conversion rates are low, the company may need to enhance its user experience or optimize its product listings.

Another critical aspect of monitoring strategies is gathering qualitative data through feedback from stakeholders. This includes employees, customers, suppliers, and partners. Surveys, interviews, and focus groups can provide valuable insights into how well the strategy is being implemented and perceived. For instance, a manufacturing company might conduct employee surveys to understand how well new efficiency protocols are being adopted on the factory floor. Feedback from employees can highlight practical challenges and areas where additional training or resources are needed.

It is also important to benchmark performance against competitors and industry standards. This external perspective helps organizations understand their relative position in the market and identify best practices that can be adopted. For example, a financial services firm might compare its customer satisfaction scores with industry averages to determine whether its service levels are competitive. If the firm finds that it lags behind its peers, it can investigate the reasons and take corrective actions, such as improving customer support or streamlining processes.

Once data is collected and analyzed, the next step is to interpret the findings and make informed decisions. This requires a combination of quantitative analysis and qualitative judgment. For example, a technology company analyzing its product development cycle might find that while most projects are completed on time, customer satisfaction with new products is declining. Further investigation may reveal that the speed of development is compromising quality. This insight would prompt the company to adjust its strategy by perhaps extending development timelines to ensure higher quality.

Adjusting strategies involves making changes based on the insights gained from monitoring. These adjustments can be minor tweaks or significant shifts, depending on the nature and magnitude of the issues identified. For instance, a non-profit organization aiming to increase donations might find through monitoring that its current donor outreach is not resonating with its target audience. An adjustment might involve redesigning the outreach campaign with a new messaging strategy or targeting different donor segments.

Flexibility and agility are key in this phase. Organizations must be willing to pivot and adapt quickly to new information and changing circumstances. For example, during the COVID-19 pandemic, many businesses had to rapidly adjust their strategies to cope with lockdowns and changing consumer behaviors. Restaurants, for instance, shifted focus from in-house dining to takeout and delivery services, often implementing new online ordering systems and contactless delivery options. Those that monitored the evolving situation closely and adjusted promptly were better able to sustain operations and serve their customers.

Effective communication is crucial when making strategic adjustments. All stakeholders must be informed about the changes and understand the reasons behind them. Clear communication helps ensure buy-in and smooth implementation. For example, if a company decides to change its product pricing strategy, it needs to communicate the rationale to its sales team, marketing department, and even customers. This might involve internal meetings, training sessions, and customer announcements to explain the benefits and expected outcomes of the new pricing approach.

A real-world example of successful monitoring and adjustment can be seen in the case of Netflix. Originally a DVD rental service, Netflix closely monitored market trends and consumer behaviors, noticing the increasing preference for online streaming. The company adjusted its strategy by investing heavily in its streaming platform and original content production. This strategic pivot allowed Netflix to become a dominant player in the digital entertainment industry, illustrating the importance of being responsive to market changes.

In contrast, the failure to monitor and adjust strategies can have dire consequences. Consider the case of Blockbuster, which did not adequately respond to the same market shifts that Netflix capitalized on. Despite having the resources and brand recognition, Blockbuster's reluctance to shift from its traditional rental model to a digital one led to its decline. This example underscores the critical need for continuous monitoring and the willingness to make strategic adjustments.

For smaller businesses, the principles of monitoring and adjusting strategies are equally applicable. A local bakery, for instance, might notice through sales data that certain products are consistently underperforming. By gathering customer feedback, the bakery might learn that these products do not meet consumer preferences. An adjustment could involve revising the product recipes or introducing new items based on customer suggestions. Additionally, the bakery could monitor trends in the food industry to innovate and stay relevant.

In practice, setting up a robust monitoring system involves several steps. First, define the objectives and identify the appropriate KPIs. Next, establish a regular reporting and review schedule, such as monthly or quarterly reviews. Use dashboards and analytics tools to visualize data and make it accessible for decision-makers. Encourage a culture of continuous improvement where feedback is valued, and adjustments are seen as opportunities for growth rather than failures.

In conclusion, monitoring and adjusting strategies are fundamental to the success and sustainability of any organization. By setting clear metrics, gathering comprehensive data, and being willing to adapt, organizations can navigate the complexities of the market and achieve their strategic goals. This dynamic approach not only addresses current challenges but also positions organizations to seize new opportunities and drive long-term success. Through effective monitoring and timely adjustments, companies can maintain their competitive edge and thrive in an ever-changing environment.

Moreover, integrating technology can significantly enhance the monitoring and adjustment process. Advanced analytics, artificial intelligence, and machine learning can provide deeper insights and predictive capabilities that were previously unattainable. For instance, a retail company can use machine learning algorithms to predict sales trends based on historical data, seasonal patterns, and external factors like economic conditions. These predictive insights allow the company to adjust inventory levels, marketing strategies, and staffing needs accordingly, preventing stockouts or overstock situations.

Chapter 4

Innovation and Business Growth

Fostering an Innovative Culture

Innovation is the lifeblood of any organization seeking to thrive in today's fast-paced world. Fostering an innovative culture requires a deliberate and strategic approach that encourages creativity, embraces risk, and values diverse perspectives. To build such a culture, leadership must spearhead initiatives that inspire employees to think outside the box and provide a supportive environment where novel ideas can flourish.

Creating an innovative culture begins with leadership's vision. Leaders must clearly articulate the importance of innovation to the organization's success and consistently communicate this vision. They should embody the principles of innovation by being open to new ideas, showing a willingness to experiment, and demonstrating resilience when faced with setbacks. For instance, when Howard Schultz returned to Starbucks as CEO, he reinvigorated the company by championing innovation in both product offerings and customer experience, setting a clear example from the top.

A crucial aspect of fostering innovation is establishing a safe environment where employees feel comfortable sharing their ideas without fear of ridicule or retribution. Psychological safety, as coined by

Harvard Business School professor Amy Edmondson, is fundamental. When employees trust that their contributions are valued and that they won't be punished for taking risks, they are more likely to propose creative solutions. This can be achieved by encouraging open dialogue, celebrating efforts regardless of their outcome, and treating failures as learning opportunities.

Diverse teams are often more innovative due to the variety of perspectives they bring. Organizations should strive to build teams with diverse backgrounds, skills, and experiences. Diversity can stimulate creativity by combining different viewpoints and approaches to problem-solving. For example, a tech company might benefit from having a team composed of engineers, designers, and marketers working together on a new product. Each member's unique perspective can lead to more comprehensive and innovative solutions.

Moreover, fostering an innovative culture involves providing employees with the resources and time to explore new ideas. Google's famous "20% time" policy, which allows employees to spend one-fifth of their workweek on projects they are passionate about, is a well-known example. This policy has led to the development of several successful products, including Gmail and Google News. By allocating time and resources for experimentation, organizations can tap into their employees' creative potential.

Recognition and rewards play a significant role in encouraging innovation. When employees see that their innovative efforts are acknowledged and rewarded, they are more likely to continue contributing creatively. This can be done through formal recognition programs, monetary incentives, or simply by publicly praising innovative ideas. For instance, Adobe's "Kickbox" initiative provides employees with a physical box containing resources, including a prepaid credit card, to experiment with new ideas. This not only empowers employees but also signals the company's commitment to innovation.

Collaboration and cross-pollination of ideas are also essential for an innovative culture. Creating spaces and opportunities for employees to collaborate across departments can lead to the exchange of ideas and the birth of innovation. Hackathons, innovation labs, and cross-functional projects are effective ways to facilitate this. For example, IBM's "Innovation Jam" brings together employees, customers, and partners to brainstorm and develop new ideas collaboratively, resulting in a multitude of innovative solutions.

Continuous learning is a cornerstone of innovation. Organizations should invest in the ongoing development of their employees through training, workshops, and access to educational resources. Encouraging a growth mindset, where employees see challenges as opportunities to learn and grow, can significantly enhance their capacity for innovation. For example, companies like Amazon and Microsoft offer extensive learning programs to keep their employees updated with the latest technologies and industry trends, fostering a culture of perpetual innovation.

Empowering employees with autonomy can also spur innovation. When employees have the freedom to make decisions and take ownership of their projects, they are more likely to experiment and innovate. This requires a shift from micromanagement to a more trust-based management style. Leaders should set clear goals and provide the necessary support, but allow employees the latitude to determine how best to achieve those goals. For instance, Netflix's culture of "Freedom and Responsibility" empowers employees to take initiative and innovate without being bogged down by excessive rules or oversight.

Innovation often stems from a deep understanding of customer needs and pain points. Organizations should cultivate a customer-centric mindset, encouraging employees to engage with customers and gather insights firsthand. This can be done through regular customer feedback sessions, surveys, and direct interactions. For example, Procter & Gamble's "Connect + Develop" program actively involves customers in the innovation process, leading to the creation of products that better meet consumer needs.

Creating an innovative culture is not a one-time effort but an ongoing journey. It requires sustained commitment and continuous evaluation of the strategies in place. Organizations should regularly assess their innovation culture through surveys, feedback, and performance metrics to identify areas for improvement. This iterative process ensures that the culture evolves and adapts to new challenges and opportunities.

Storytelling can be a powerful tool in fostering an innovative culture. Sharing stories of successful innovations, whether from within the organization or from external sources, can inspire and motivate employees. These stories can highlight the journey of innovation, including the challenges faced and the breakthroughs achieved, demonstrating that innovation is a rewarding yet challenging endeavor. For instance, 3M's story of the Post-it Note, which began as a failed adhesive experiment, serves as an inspirational tale of perseverance and creative thinking.

Ultimately, fostering an innovative culture requires a holistic approach that permeates every aspect of the organization. It involves leadership commitment, a supportive environment, diverse and collaborative teams, continuous learning, and a customer-centric focus. By embedding these principles into the organizational DNA, companies can create a fertile ground for innovation to thrive, ensuring long-term success and sustainability in an ever-changing world.

Innovation is not just about coming up with new ideas; it's about creating an environment where those ideas can be nurtured, tested, and implemented. It's about encouraging employees to think differently, take risks, and learn from their experiences. By fostering an innovative culture, organizations can unlock their full potential, drive growth, and stay ahead of the competition.

Building a culture of innovation relies on a few additional key elements: fostering open communication, leveraging external partnerships, and integrating innovation into the organizational strategy.

Identifying Growth Opportunities

Identifying growth opportunities is a crucial skill for any business seeking to expand and thrive in a competitive market. Growth does not happen by accident; it requires a keen eye for potential, strategic planning, and the ability to seize opportunities as they arise. To identify these opportunities effectively, businesses need to employ a combination of market analysis, customer insights, and internal assessments.

Market analysis is the foundation of identifying growth opportunities. It involves understanding the broader economic landscape, industry trends, and the competitive environment. Businesses should begin by examining macroeconomic indicators such as GDP growth, inflation rates, and consumer spending patterns. These indicators can provide a sense of the overall economic climate and potential areas for expansion. For example, during periods of economic growth, consumers may have more disposable income, which could lead to increased demand for luxury goods or non-essential services.

Industry trends are equally important. Keeping an eye on technological advancements, regulatory changes, and shifts in consumer behavior can reveal new opportunities. For instance, the rise of e-commerce has created vast opportunities for businesses to reach customers globally. Companies that recognized this trend early, like Amazon, leveraged it to grow exponentially. Similarly, the increasing focus on sustainability has opened up new markets for eco-friendly products and services. Businesses that anticipate and adapt to these trends can position themselves advantageously in the market.

Competitive analysis is another critical component. By evaluating the strengths and weaknesses of competitors, businesses can identify gaps in the market that they can exploit. This involves looking at competitors' product offerings, pricing strategies, marketing tactics, and customer feedback. For example, if competitors are neglecting a particular segment of the market, this might present an opportunity for a business to step in and meet the needs of those customers. Additionally, understanding competitors' weaknesses can help businesses differentiate themselves and offer superior value.

Customer insights are invaluable in identifying growth opportunities. Businesses should engage directly with their customers to understand their needs, preferences, and pain points. This can be done through surveys, focus groups, and direct feedback channels. For example, a software company might discover through customer feedback that users are looking for a mobile version of their product. By developing and launching a mobile app, the company can tap into a new customer base and drive growth.

Internal assessments are also crucial. Businesses need to evaluate their own strengths and capabilities to identify areas where they can grow. This involves looking at existing resources, core competencies, and operational efficiencies. For example, a company with strong research and development capabilities might identify growth opportunities in innovation and new product development. Alternatively, a business with efficient supply chain operations might explore opportunities in expanding distribution channels or entering new geographic markets.

Strategic partnerships and alliances can open up new growth opportunities. By collaborating with other businesses, companies can leverage complementary strengths and access new markets. For instance, a small tech startup might partner with a larger company to gain access to their distribution network and customer base. These partnerships can provide the resources and market presence needed to drive growth.

Diversification is another strategy for identifying growth opportunities. This involves expanding into new products, services, or markets that are different from the current business offerings. Diversification can help businesses reduce risk and tap into new revenue streams. For example, a company that manufactures household appliances might diversify into smart home technology, capitalizing on the growing trend of connected devices.

Innovation is at the heart of growth. Businesses should foster a culture of innovation where employees are encouraged to come up with new ideas and solutions. This can be achieved through regular brainstorming sessions, innovation workshops, and providing resources for experimentation. For example, 3M has a long-standing practice of allowing employees to spend a portion of their time on projects of their choosing, which has led to the development of successful products like Post-it Notes and Scotchgard.

Entering new markets is a powerful growth strategy. This could involve expanding into new geographic regions or targeting new customer segments. Before entering a new market, businesses should conduct thorough market research to understand the local conditions, customer preferences, and regulatory environment. For example, a beverage company looking to expand into a new country should assess local tastes, distribution channels, and any legal requirements related to food and beverage products.

Leveraging digital transformation can also unlock growth opportunities. The rise of digital technologies has transformed how businesses operate and engage with customers. By embracing digital tools and platforms, businesses can streamline operations, enhance customer experiences, and open up new revenue streams. For example, a retail business might develop an e-commerce platform to reach customers online, or a service provider might use digital marketing to target specific customer segments more effectively.

Mergers and acquisitions (M&A) are another way to identify and capitalize on growth opportunities. Acquiring or merging with another company can provide immediate access to new markets, technologies, and customer bases. However, M&A activities require careful due diligence and strategic planning to ensure alignment with the business's overall growth objectives. For instance, Disney's acquisition of Pixar allowed it to revitalize its animation division and produce a string of successful films.

Investing in talent and skills development is essential for sustainable growth. Businesses should ensure that their workforce has the necessary skills and expertise to drive innovation and expansion. This might involve training programs, leadership development initiatives, and attracting top talent from the industry. For example, investing in data analytics skills can enable a business to make more informed decisions and identify growth opportunities through data-driven insights.

Finally, businesses should continuously monitor and adapt their growth strategies. The market environment is dynamic, and opportunities can arise or disappear rapidly. By maintaining a flexible and responsive approach, businesses can quickly pivot and capitalize on emerging opportunities. Regularly reviewing performance metrics, market conditions, and strategic objectives can help businesses stay on track and adjust their plans as needed.

In conclusion, identifying growth opportunities requires a comprehensive and proactive approach. By combining market analysis, customer insights, internal assessments, strategic partnerships, diversification, innovation, market expansion, digital transformation, M&A activities, and talent investment, businesses can uncover and capitalize on opportunities for growth. Maintaining flexibility and continuously adapting to the changing market landscape are crucial for sustained success. Through diligent effort and strategic planning, businesses can position themselves to seize growth opportunities and achieve long-term prosperity.

Monitoring and harnessing technological advancements can create significant growth opportunities for businesses. Staying abreast of emerging technologies, such as artificial intelligence, blockchain, and the Internet of Things (IoT), allows companies to innovate their products, services, and internal processes. For example, a logistics company that adopts IoT devices can improve its supply chain efficiency through real-time tracking and predictive maintenance, reducing costs and enhancing service reliability.

Product Development Strategies

Product development strategies are essential for any business aiming to innovate and stay competitive in a fast-paced market. A well-crafted product development strategy not only helps in bringing new products to market but also ensures that these products meet customer needs and drive business growth. The journey from concept to market involves several stages, each demanding meticulous planning, creativity, and execution.

The first step in developing a successful product is identifying a market need or opportunity. This can be achieved through various methods such as market research, customer feedback, or analyzing industry trends. For instance, Henry Ford famously noted that if he had asked people what they wanted, they would have said faster horses. Instead, he identified a need for more efficient transportation and developed the automobile. This example illustrates the importance of looking beyond immediate customer demands to understand underlying needs and potential innovations.

Once a market need is identified, the next phase is idea generation. This stage involves brainstorming and generating a wide range of ideas that could potentially address the identified need. Encouraging a culture of creativity within the organization is crucial during this phase. Techniques such as mind mapping, SWOT analysis (Strengths, Weaknesses, Opportunities, Threats), and competitive analysis can be valuable tools. Additionally, involving cross-functional teams can bring diverse perspectives and foster innovative solutions.

After generating a pool of ideas, the next crucial step is idea screening. Not all ideas will be feasible or aligned with the company's strategic goals. Therefore, it is essential to evaluate each idea against specific criteria such as market potential, technical feasibility, and alignment with the company's core competencies. This screening process helps in narrowing down the ideas to those with the highest potential for success. For example, Google is known for its rigorous idea screening process, where only a small fraction of ideas make it past the initial evaluation phase.

Once the best ideas are selected, the next step is concept development and testing. This involves creating detailed product concepts and testing them with potential customers to gather feedback. Concept testing can help validate assumptions, identify potential flaws, and refine product features. Techniques such as surveys, focus groups, and prototype testing are commonly used during this phase. For example, before launching the iPhone, Apple created multiple prototypes and conducted extensive user testing to ensure a seamless user experience.

Following successful concept testing, the next stage is business analysis. This involves assessing the financial viability of the product. Key considerations include projected sales, cost estimates, pricing strategies, and profitability analysis. A detailed business plan is developed, outlining the product's market potential, competitive landscape, marketing strategy, and financial projections. This phase ensures that the product aligns with the company's financial goals and resources.

With a solid business plan in place, the next step is product development. This phase involves turning the product concept into a tangible product. It requires close collaboration between various departments such as research and development, engineering, design, and manufacturing. Agile development methodologies, which emphasize iterative progress and continuous feedback, can be particularly effective in this phase. For example, software companies like Microsoft and Adobe use agile development to rapidly develop and refine their products based on user feedback.

Parallel to product development, businesses should also focus on creating a comprehensive marketing strategy. This includes defining the target market, positioning the product, and developing a marketing mix (product, price, place, promotion). Effective marketing strategies often leverage digital marketing, social media, content marketing, and traditional advertising channels. For instance, Nike's marketing strategy for new product launches involves high-profile endorsements, social media campaigns, and immersive brand experiences to create buzz and drive sales.

As the product nears completion, the next phase is market testing. This involves launching the product on a limited scale to test all aspects of the product and marketing strategy. Market testing can help identify any issues that need to be addressed before a full-scale launch. Techniques such as beta testing, test markets, and pilot launches are commonly used. For example, fast-food chains often test new menu items in select locations to gauge customer response before rolling them out nationwide.

After successful market testing, the final phase is commercialization. This involves launching the product on a full scale and implementing the marketing strategy. Key activities include mass production, distribution, sales training, and promotional campaigns. Effective project management and coordination are crucial during this phase to ensure a smooth launch. For instance, the launch of Tesla's Model 3 involved meticulous planning and coordination across production, marketing, and customer service teams to meet high demand and deliver a seamless customer experience.

Post-launch, it is essential to continuously monitor the product's performance and gather customer feedback. This helps in identifying any issues, improving the product, and making informed decisions for future product development. Techniques such as customer surveys, product reviews, and social media monitoring can provide valuable insights. For example, Amazon continuously gathers customer feedback to refine its products and services, ensuring they meet evolving customer needs.

In addition to these steps, businesses should also focus on fostering a culture of continuous improvement. This involves regularly reviewing and refining product development processes, encouraging innovation, and staying abreast of industry trends and technological advancements. Companies like Toyota have successfully implemented continuous improvement practices, known as Kaizen, to enhance product quality and operational efficiency.

Collaboration and partnerships can also play a vital role in successful product development. Partnering with other companies, research institutions, or technology providers can bring in additional expertise, resources, and market access. For instance, pharmaceutical companies often collaborate with research institutions to develop new drugs, combining their expertise in drug development with cutting-edge scientific research.

Finally, businesses should invest in developing the skills and capabilities of their product development teams. This includes providing training, fostering a collaborative work environment, and encouraging professional development. A skilled and motivated team is essential for driving innovation and successfully bringing new products to market.

In conclusion, effective product development strategies involve a systematic approach that includes identifying market needs, generating and screening ideas, developing and testing concepts, conducting business analysis, and executing a comprehensive marketing and commercialization plan. Continuous improvement, collaboration, and investment in team capabilities are also crucial for sustained success. By meticulously following these steps and fostering a culture of innovation, businesses can develop products that meet customer needs, drive growth, and maintain a competitive edge in the market.

Maintaining a competitive edge in product development also requires businesses to stay agile and adaptable. The market landscape is continually evolving, influenced by technological advancements, changing consumer preferences, and global economic shifts. Companies must be prepared to pivot their strategies and iterate on their products based on new data and insights.

Expanding into New Markets

Expanding into new markets is a critical growth strategy for businesses seeking to diversify their revenue streams and reduce dependency on existing markets. This process, however, is fraught with challenges and requires careful planning, research, and execution. Companies must navigate cultural differences, regulatory environments, and competitive landscapes to succeed. Here's a comprehensive guide to help you strategically expand into new markets.

The first step in market expansion is conducting thorough market research. This involves identifying potential markets that align with your business goals and understanding their unique characteristics. Market research can be conducted through various methods such as surveys, focus groups, and analyzing secondary data sources. For instance, when Starbucks decided to enter the Chinese market, they conducted extensive research to understand local consumer preferences, competitive dynamics, and cultural nuances. This research helped them tailor their offerings to suit the local palate and establish a strong foothold in China.

Understanding the cultural context of the new market is crucial. Cultural differences can significantly impact consumer behavior and preferences. Businesses must adapt their products, marketing strategies, and customer service to resonate with the local culture. For example, McDonald's has successfully expanded into numerous markets by adapting its menu to local tastes. In India, where a significant portion of the population is vegetarian, McDonald's introduced a range of vegetarian options, ensuring that their offerings were culturally appropriate and appealing to local consumers.

Regulatory compliance is another critical aspect of market expansion. Different countries have varying regulations related to product standards, advertising, labor laws, and more. It is essential to understand and comply with these regulations to avoid legal issues and ensure smooth operations. For example, when Uber expanded into European markets, they faced numerous regulatory challenges related to labor laws and licensing requirements. Navigating these regulations required significant legal expertise and adjustments to their business model.

Selecting the right market entry strategy is also crucial for successful expansion. There are several entry modes to consider, each with its advantages and disadvantages. These include exporting, licensing, franchising, joint ventures, and wholly-owned subsidiaries. The choice of entry mode depends on factors such as the level of control desired, resource availability, and market conditions. For instance, IKEA often uses joint ventures when entering new markets to leverage local partners' knowledge and resources while maintaining control over their brand and operations.

Building a local team or partnering with local businesses can provide invaluable insights and operational support. Local employees and partners have a better understanding of the market and can help navigate cultural and regulatory complexities. They can also facilitate connections with local suppliers, distributors, and customers. For example, when Walmart entered the Mexican market, they partnered with Cifra, a local retail chain, which provided them with valuable market knowledge and an established distribution network.

Developing a localization strategy is essential for catering to the unique needs and preferences of the new market. This involves adapting your product, marketing, and customer service to align with local tastes and expectations. Localization goes beyond mere translation; it includes modifying product features, packaging, pricing, and promotional strategies to resonate with local consumers. For instance, Coca-Cola uses localized advertising campaigns that reflect the cultural values and traditions of each market they operate in, ensuring that their brand feels familiar and relevant to local consumers.

Pricing strategy plays a crucial role in market expansion. The pricing should reflect local purchasing power, competitive pricing, and perceived value. Conducting a thorough analysis of local pricing dynamics and consumer behavior can help you set competitive prices that attract customers while ensuring profitability. For example, Apple adjusts its pricing strategy based on the economic conditions and competitive landscape of each market, balancing affordability with the premium positioning of their products.

Effective marketing and branding are essential for establishing a strong presence in the new market. Tailoring your marketing messages to resonate with local consumers and leveraging appropriate marketing channels can enhance brand visibility and customer engagement. Digital marketing, social media, and influencer partnerships are particularly effective in reaching and engaging local audiences. For instance, when entering the Indian market, Netflix collaborated with popular local influencers and produced content that catered to Indian audiences' preferences, significantly boosting their subscriber base.

Distribution and logistics are critical components of market expansion. Ensuring that your products are available at the right place and time requires a well-planned distribution strategy. This may involve setting up local warehouses, partnering with local distributors, or developing an efficient supply chain network. For example, Amazon invested heavily in building an extensive logistics network in India, including local warehouses and a robust delivery system, to ensure fast and reliable delivery of products to Indian consumers.

Monitoring and evaluating the performance of your market expansion efforts is crucial for continuous improvement. Establishing key performance indicators (KPIs) such as sales growth, market share, customer satisfaction, and profitability can help you track progress and identify areas for improvement. Regularly reviewing these metrics and gathering feedback from local customers and partners can provide valuable insights for refining your strategies and achieving long-term success in the new market.

Managing risks associated with market expansion is essential for protecting your investment and ensuring sustainable growth. This involves identifying potential risks such as political instability, economic fluctuations, and competitive threats, and developing contingency plans to mitigate these risks. For instance, companies expanding into emerging markets often face higher risks due to volatile economic and political conditions. Developing a risk management framework that includes diversification strategies, insurance, and crisis management plans can help mitigate these risks and safeguard your business.

Investing in technology and innovation can also enhance your market expansion efforts. Leveraging digital tools and technologies such as e-commerce platforms, data analytics, and customer relationship management (CRM) systems can streamline operations, enhance customer experiences, and provide valuable insights into market trends and consumer behavior. For example, Zara uses advanced data analytics and a responsive supply chain to quickly adapt to changing fashion trends and customer preferences in different markets, ensuring that they remain competitive and relevant.

Building strong relationships with local stakeholders is essential for gaining support and ensuring smooth operations in the new market. This includes engaging with local government authorities, industry associations, community leaders, and customers. Developing a positive reputation and demonstrating a commitment to the local community can enhance your brand image and foster goodwill. For example, Starbucks engages in various community initiatives and sustainability programs in the markets they operate in, building strong relationships with local stakeholders and enhancing their brand reputation.

In conclusion, expanding into new markets requires a strategic and multifaceted approach that includes thorough market research, cultural adaptation, regulatory compliance, selecting the right entry strategy, building local partnerships, developing a localization strategy, effective marketing and distribution, performance monitoring, risk management, leveraging technology, and building strong relationships with local stakeholders. By carefully planning and executing these steps, businesses can successfully navigate the complexities of market expansion and achieve sustainable growth in new markets.

Navigating the competitive landscape in new markets is another critical aspect of successful expansion. Understanding who your competitors are, what they offer, and how they position themselves can provide valuable insights for differentiating your own products or services. Conducting a competitive analysis involves assessing competitors' strengths and weaknesses, market share, pricing strategies, customer base, and marketing tactics. For example, when Tesla expanded into the Chinese market, they closely studied local electric vehicle manufacturers and strategically positioned their vehicles as premium products with superior technology and performance.

Scaling Operations

Scaling operations is a transformative phase in a business's lifecycle, marking the transition from a startup to a more mature entity capable of sustaining larger volumes of production, sales, and customer service. This process involves expanding your operational capacity while maintaining or improving efficiency and quality. It requires meticulous planning, robust systems, and a scalable business model. Here's a comprehensive guide to successfully scale your operations.

The foundation of scaling operations lies in a clear understanding of your current processes and their limitations. Conduct a thorough audit of your existing operations to identify bottlenecks, inefficiencies, and areas for improvement. This audit should cover every aspect of your operations, from production and supply chain management to sales and customer service. For example, when Amazon began to scale, they meticulously analyzed their warehousing and distribution processes, identifying key areas where automation and technology could enhance efficiency.

Investing in technology is often a critical component of scaling operations. Automation, data analytics, and cloud computing are just a few of the technologies that can significantly enhance operational efficiency. Automation can streamline repetitive tasks, reduce errors, and free up human resources for more strategic activities. Data analytics can provide valuable insights into operational performance, customer behavior, and market trends, enabling more informed decision-making. Cloud computing offers scalability, flexibility, and cost savings by allowing businesses to easily scale their IT infrastructure as needed. For example, using advanced manufacturing systems and robotics has enabled companies like Tesla to scale their production capabilities while maintaining high levels of precision and efficiency.

Building a robust supply chain is essential for scaling operations. As your business grows, so does the complexity of your supply chain. It's crucial to establish strong relationships with reliable suppliers and develop a resilient supply chain that can adapt to changes in demand and market conditions. This may involve diversifying your supplier base, investing in supply chain management software, and implementing just-in-time inventory systems to reduce waste and improve efficiency. For instance, Apple has developed a highly efficient and flexible supply chain that allows them to quickly respond to changes in consumer demand and market conditions.

Expanding your production capacity is often necessary to support increased demand. This can be achieved through various means, such as investing in new facilities, upgrading existing equipment, or outsourcing production to third-party manufacturers. When expanding production capacity, it's important to consider factors such as location, cost, and scalability. For example, Nike has strategically located its manufacturing facilities around the world to optimize production costs and ensure timely delivery of products to various markets.

Hiring and retaining skilled talent is crucial for scaling operations. As your business grows, you'll need to expand your workforce to support increased production, sales, and customer service. It's important to develop a comprehensive talent acquisition strategy that includes attracting top talent, providing competitive compensation and benefits, and fostering a positive workplace culture. Additionally, investing in employee training and development can enhance skills and productivity, enabling your team to effectively support your scaling efforts. For instance, Google invests heavily in employee development programs, which have helped them build a highly skilled and motivated workforce capable of driving innovation and growth.

Developing scalable processes and systems is essential for supporting growth. This involves standardizing procedures, implementing robust quality control measures, and establishing clear communication channels. Standardized processes can enhance efficiency, reduce errors, and ensure consistent quality across all aspects of your operations. Quality control measures, such as regular inspections and audits, can help maintain high standards and prevent defects. Clear communication channels can facilitate collaboration and coordination among teams, ensuring that everyone is aligned and working towards common goals. For example, McDonald's has developed highly standardized processes and quality control measures that enable them to consistently deliver high-quality products and services across thousands of locations worldwide.

Financial management is a critical aspect of scaling operations. As your business grows, so do your financial needs. It's important to develop a comprehensive financial plan that includes budgeting, forecasting, and cash flow management. This plan should outline your financial goals, identify potential sources of funding, and establish a framework for monitoring and controlling expenses. Additionally, implementing robust financial management systems can provide real-time insights into your financial performance, enabling you to make more informed decisions and effectively manage your resources. For instance, Salesforce has developed a highly sophisticated financial management system that allows them to monitor their financial performance in real-time and make data-driven decisions that support their growth objectives.

Customer satisfaction should remain a top priority as you scale your operations. Maintaining high levels of customer satisfaction can enhance loyalty, drive repeat business, and generate positive word-of-mouth. This involves delivering high-quality products and services, providing exceptional customer service, and actively seeking and responding to customer feedback. Implementing customer relationship management (CRM) systems can help you effectively manage customer interactions, track customer preferences, and personalize your offerings. For example, Zappos has built a reputation for exceptional customer service by prioritizing customer satisfaction and using CRM systems to deliver personalized and responsive service.

Innovation and continuous improvement are key to sustaining growth. As your business scales, it's important to foster a culture of innovation and encourage continuous improvement. This involves regularly evaluating your processes, seeking new ways to enhance efficiency and quality, and staying abreast of industry trends and technological advancements. Encouraging a culture of innovation can inspire your team to develop creative solutions and drive continuous improvement. For instance, Toyota has implemented a continuous improvement philosophy known as Kaizen, which involves regularly evaluating and improving their processes to enhance efficiency and quality.

Risk management is an essential aspect of scaling operations. As your business grows, you may face new risks and challenges, such as supply chain disruptions, regulatory changes, and increased competition. It's important to develop a comprehensive risk management plan that identifies potential risks, assesses their impact, and establishes strategies for mitigating them. This may involve diversifying your supplier base, implementing robust compliance programs, and developing contingency plans for potential disruptions. For example, Johnson & Johnson has developed a comprehensive risk management framework that enables them to identify and mitigate risks across their global operations, ensuring business continuity and resilience.

Leveraging partnerships and collaborations can also support your scaling efforts. Partnering with other businesses, industry associations, and research institutions can provide access to new resources, expertise, and markets. Collaborations can enhance your capabilities, drive innovation, and create new growth opportunities. For instance, Pfizer has leveraged partnerships with research institutions and other pharmaceutical companies to accelerate the development and commercialization of new drugs, enhancing their ability to scale their operations and drive growth.

Effective communication and leadership are critical for successful scaling. Clear communication ensures that everyone in your organization understands the goals, strategies, and expectations. Strong leadership provides direction, motivates your team, and drives execution. It's important to develop a communication strategy that includes regular updates, transparent reporting, and opportunities for feedback. Additionally, investing in leadership development can enhance your leaders' ability to effectively guide and support your scaling efforts. For example, General Electric (GE) has developed a comprehensive leadership development program that cultivates strong leaders capable of driving growth and innovation.

In conclusion, scaling operations requires a strategic and multifaceted approach that involves auditing existing processes, investing in technology, building a robust supply chain, expanding production capacity, hiring and retaining skilled talent, developing scalable processes, managing finances, prioritizing customer satisfaction, fostering innovation, managing risks, leveraging partnerships, and ensuring effective communication and leadership. By carefully planning and executing these steps, businesses can successfully scale their operations, enhance efficiency and quality, and drive sustainable growth. The journey of scaling operations is complex and challenging, but with the right strategies and mindset, businesses can achieve remarkable growth and success.

It's also important to consider the role of company culture in the scaling process. As your business grows, maintaining a cohesive and positive company culture can be challenging but is crucial for long-term success. A strong culture can drive employee engagement, retention, and productivity, while also attracting top talent who resonate with your company's values and mission. To preserve and nurture your culture, clearly define your core values, communicate them consistently, and integrate them into every aspect of your operations, from hiring and onboarding to performance evaluations and daily interactions. For example, Patagonia has successfully scaled its operations while maintaining a strong commitment to environmental sustainability and social responsibility, which are core to its company culture.